# LITERACIES, EXPERIENCES, AND TECHNOLOGIES

## REFLECTIVE PRACTICES OF AN ALIEN RESEARCHER

**NEW DIMENSIONS IN COMPUTERS AND COMPOSITION**

Gail E. Hawisher and Cynthia L. Selfe, editors

Digital Youth: Emerging Literacies on the World Wide Web
*Jonathan Alexander*

Role Play: Distance Learning and the Teaching of Writing
*Jonathan Alexander and Marcia Dickson* (eds.)

Aging Literacies: Training and Development Challenges for Faculty
*Angela Crow*

Writing Community Change: Designing Technologies for Citizen Action
*Jeffrey T. Grabill*

Literacies, Experiences and Technologies: Reflective Practices of an Alien Researcher
*Sibylle Gruber*

Datacloud: Toward a New Theory of Online Work
*Johndan Johnson-Eilola*

Digital Writing Research: Technologies, Methodologies and Ethical Issues
*Heidi A. McKee and Danielle DeVoss* (eds.)

At Play in the Fields of Writing: A Serio-Ludic Rhetoric
*Albert Rouzie*

Integrating Hypertextual Subjects: Computers, Composition, Critical Literacy and Academic Labor
*Robert Samuels*

Multimodal Composition Resources for Teachers
*Cynthia L. Selfe* (ed.)

Sustainable Computer Environments: Cultures of Support in English Studies and Language Arts
*Richard Selfe*

Doing Literacy Online: Teaching, Learning, and Playing in an Electronic World
*Ilana Snyder and Catherine Beavis* (eds.)

Labor, Writing Technologies and the Shaping of Composition in the Academy
*Pamela Takayoshi and Patricia Sullivan* (eds.)

*forthcoming*

Webbing Cyberfeminine Practice: Communities, Pedagogy and Social Action
*Kristine Blair, Radhika Gajjala,* and *Christine Tully* (eds.)

Going Wireless: A Critical Exploration of Wireless and Mobile Technologies for Composition Teachers and Scholars
*Amy C. Kimme Hea*

# LITERACIES, EXPERIENCES, AND TECHNOLOGIES

## REFLECTIVE PRACTICES OF AN ALIEN RESEARCHER

**Sibylle Gruber**
*Northern Arizona University*

HAMPTON PRESS, INC.
CRESSKILL, NEW JERSEY

Printed in the United States of America

Library of Congress Cataloging-in-Publication Data

Gruber, Sibylle
Literacies, experiences, and technologies : reflective practices of an alien researcher / Sibylle Gruber
p. cm. -- (New dimensions in computers and composition)
Includes bibliographic references and index.
ISBN 1-57273-703-4 (hardbound) -- ISBN 1-57273-704-2 (paperbound)
1. Language arts--Computer assisted instruction. 2. English language--Computer assisted instruction. 3. Computers and literacy. 4. Minorities--Education (Higher)--United States. I. Title.
LB1576.7G78 2007
428.0078'5--dc22

2007006536

Hampton Press, Inc.
23 Broadway
Cresskill, NJ 07626

Für meine Familie

Anna Alois
Maria Hans Lois Ernst Josef
Christine Mary Petra
Eva-Maria Raphaela Johnny Theresa Samuel Jakob
Nancy
Cleopatra

# CONTENTS

# ACKNOWLEDGEMENTS

When I started this project, I didn't know how much I would learn, and how much I still need to learn. I know that this book could be rewritten many times over, and I take full responsibility for any shortcomings. But I know it has come a long way because of those who helped me along the way.

Gail Hawisher and Cynthia Selfe have been my greatest supporters and friends for many years. They have been my all-time favorite mentors. They never tired of my questions, helped me in my professional career, gave me wonderful advice, were enthusiastic about my project, and have always encouraged me to do my best.

Nancy G. Barron has pushed me to think more critically about my own identity and my place in the United States. I would not have been able to write this book without her valuable input and her insights, and her pointed questions about why I thought the way I did, why I wrote about the topics I wrote about, and why I used the theories I used. Because of her, I now have more questions to ask and more stories to write.

My colleagues at Northern Arizona University will always have a special place in my heart. They have made it easy over the last 9 years to finally hang out with Americans. I especially thank Jean Boreen who has worked with me on many projects, has been kind and considerate as a department chair and friend, has helped me succeed professionally, and has been instrumental in putting *The Sound of Music* into the right context. I thank Ann Cummins, who inspired me to be creative in my thinking, and who has immortalized my name in her latest novel. I thank Laura Gray-Rosendale who has patiently read and commented on many of my drafts. I thank Irene Matthews who has kept me focused on the important points in life. And I thank all my departmental colleagues who have supported me, rooted for my success, and humored me.

I thank everybody who has helped me in my academic career. I have worked with many wonderful colleagues over the years who have been excellent editors, who have pushed me in my thinking and in my writing, and who have been superb reviewers of my work. My writing has become stronger because of them.

Und ich danke meiner Familie. Meine Eltern waren immer für mich da obwohl sie nie verstanden haben warum ich nicht in Österreich geblieben bin. Meine Geschwister haben mich immer unterstützt und waren immer stolz auf ihre kleine Schwester. Meine Nichten und Neffen waren immer eine angenehme Abwechslung für mich. Ohne meiner Familie wäre ich nicht wer und wo ich heute bin.

And without Cleopatra Marie, I wouldn't have taken long walks with my friends, and I wouldn't have been able to talk and listen to the many stories, comments, and theories that made it possible to write *Literacies, Experiences, and Technologies*.

# 1

# ESTABLISHING NETWORKS

## LITERACIES, EXPERIENCES AND TECHNOLOGIES

When I started to publish on the impact of computer technologies on student learning, and on the importance of looking closely at students' cultural, economic, social, and gendered backgrounds, I was reluctant to address how my own status as an alien, an international, a foreigner, and an immigrant influenced my approach to research. Instead, I used postmodern theories and feminist thinking to frame my arguments. I emphasized the need to question authority, traditional patriarchal discourse patterns, domination, and hierarchies. I also wanted to make sure that my research included a strong stand on the politics of exclusion and oppression, especially when involuntary minority students were involved. I hoped to engage in inclusionary research on classroom practices that took into consideration that students' backgrounds vary, their oral selves differ from their written selves, and their online roles differ from their offline roles, replacing a singular "I" with a plural "we." I ardently believed—and still believe—in Susan Leigh Star's (1991) commentary from "Invisible Work and Silenced Dialogues": "And we are all marginal in some regard, because we are all members of more than one community of practice and thus of many networks, at the moment of action we draw together repertoires mixed from different worlds" (p. 90). In other words, I saw my role as being at the forefront of changing established research practices that had as its foundation the mythic ideal of a stable reality and unified whole. But I rarely addressed how my background influenced the conclusions I was drawing about the problems with "established practices." Instead, I was convinced that pulling from postmodern, feminist, and cyborgian theories would make my research more open-ended, would take my research participants' many realities into consideration, and would not impose a fixed reality on any of my participants, while many times assuming that my identity did not have to be part of the discussion.

I now realize that my own positionalities, my own struggles with acquiring academic literacy, and my difficulties with fitting into a U.S. system contributed to my interest in a research agenda that would acknowledge the multiple, shifting, and sometimes contradictory positions that especially minority students and women occupied in an academic setting. I wanted to look at the acquisition of academic discourse(s) and at the strategies students bring to the task. I thought it necessary to show that the use of academic discourse has to be seen in the context of students' diverse backgrounds and their immersion in various discourse conventions that often challenge traditional academic expectations. Thus, my examination of individual students' appropriation of the virtual contact zone was intended to reaffirm the need to apply critical and feminist theories to classroom contexts. In connection with these observations, I argued for valuing multiple discourses in school settings, and I proposed classroom practices that acknowledged the ambiguity and diversity in both online and face-to-face contexts. I was certain that introducing computers into classrooms had implications beyond having to learn a new technology, because not only would we have to become familiar with the technology, but we also would have to recognize the changed perceptions of reality and self created through the use of it.

As a relatively strong technology enthusiast—after initial fears and reservations about the usefulness of technology in any setting—I was excited about enriching the field of computers and composition with in-depth analyses of the potential benefits—and the possible pitfalls—of integrating computers into the field of writing. Of course, because of my training, the articles I read on this topic, and my own predilection to see computers as useful for writing influenced my research questions and the angle I took for interviewing participants, researching prior studies, and presenting my findings. In the end, like many other studies in the field, my conclusions mainly were that although there might be some pitfalls when computers are used overenthusiastically, in the end we gain more than we lose.

I am still excited about the potential uses of technology in the writing classroom. I have implemented a technology-rich curriculum in a first-year writing curriculum where students are encouraged to move from functional technological literacy to critical technological literacy. I have taught web-based courses that encourage students to form online communities and to engage in critical discussions about the topics addressed in the course. Through my day-to-day experiences in the field, however, I have become more aware of the need to mediate between theory and practice. I have learned to look more closely at my own ideological leanings and the resulting decisions I make in my teaching and administrative careers. The beliefs I hold not only influence how I apply theory, but they also influence how I understand practice. And my experiences—as an alien who came to the United States not too long ago, and as an academic in the United States—have taught me that theory is always part of my practices, and that practice is the foundation for developing new theories. Of course, in many instances, institutional restraints, in addition to the theories I find useful in my thinking about literacy, pedagogy, or research, influence how I approach teaching, scholarship, and the training of graduate assistants.

In this book, I use four case studies to show the need for a continuous self-reflective approach when we discuss the theories and practices of implementing new information technologies into existing or newly developing programs and curricula. I argue that we need to take into account the complexities of ideological beliefs, theoretical underpinnings, practical applications, and institutional constraints when we research, teach, and discuss new literacy practices. This self-reflection, as I show, is not only necessary for individual teachers, scholars, and administrators within a specific field of study, but is also necessary for the field itself. In a sense, I want to make sure that readers take to heart what Selfe and Hawisher (2004) so eloquently pointed out: "the degree to which new literacies assume importance and become accessible to particular groups and individual people, or don't, has much to do with the prevailing cultural ecology of the times: that complex intermingling of social, historical, political, and material forces within which human beings live their lives" (p. 110).

Readers of this book are encouraged to keep in mind the following questions: How do the theories we use promote specific ideological leanings, and how can they lead to new understandings or misunderstandings about students' technological literacy experiences? How do our positions as academics—teacher, scholar, administrator, advisor, or student—and as individuals from specific economic, cultural, social, historical, ethnic, racial, and gender backgrounds influence our practical and theoretical choices? How can we reflect on our practices and theories to arrive at new understandings of literacy learning in our institutions? And, how can we apply what we learned through reflecting on our practices and theories in our positions as teacher, scholar, administrator, advisor, or student? In the following chapters, I explore and reflect on my own approaches—overtly or covertly influenced by my alien status in the United States—to studying how students manage new information technologies and how the "prevailing cultural ecology of the times" (Selfe & Hawisher, 2004) influences their and my own understanding of what it means to be literate in an environment that adheres to diverse cultural, social, political, economic, racial, and gender norms. I show how my research, and my thinking about how to conduct research, developed over time, taking seriously Janet Carey Eldred's (2005) comments in *Sentimental Attachments* that "we are living drafts in progress" (p. 93). In other words, this book is an example of a researcher's attempt to listen, to learn, and to question assumptions that we carry with us when we conduct research.

Chapter 2 underscores the fundamental concept of reflecting on the theoretical principles that we use as a framework for our research. I show how my understanding of work published in the 1980s and 1990s influenced my interpretation of students' technological literacy skills that I conducted over the last 10 years. Allucquère Rosanne Stone (1995), Sherry Turkle (1984, 1996), and Donna Haraway (1990), as well as Gloria Anzaldúa (1987), Marsha Houston (1992), and Min-Zhan Lu (1999, 2001) are only a few examples I use to highlight the connections I made in my research to show how technology use can be influenced by a user's cultural background, race, gender, class, or sexual orientation. I contend that we need to be critically aware of our own subjectivities, arguing that we need to take seriously Iris Marion Young's (1997) admonition that we cannot assume symmetrical reciprocity in our relationships but that instead we need to learn about the other by mutually respecting each other and each other's worldview. Similarly, I point out that we need to take seriously Min-Zhan Lu's (1999) call for "critical affirmation" to assure that we continuously question our own predilections and ideologies.

The research studies I included in this book provide glimpses into the complexity of issues involved in interpreting the history, culture, social circumstances, and political implications surrounding the researchers and research participants' stories or written comments. Chapters 3 and 4 provide a close analysis of individual participants' interactions in an online environment, pointing out the need for carefully delineating the researcher's objectives, the complex positionalities occupied by researcher and participant, and the theoretical, ideological, and textual frameworks used to delineate participants' actions and interactions. Chapter 3 specifically addresses the role of the author, arguing for a reinterpretation of how we do research and how we talk about research. I show the assumptions I made before analyzing Alba's—a first-year Latina student—comments on race, racism, and violence in an online exchange. By interweaving my story with Alba's story, I also show how my ideologies, my histories, politics, cultural background, economics, and international status influenced my reading and my interpretation of Alba's face-to-face and online comments.

Similarly, Chapter 4 shows the need to carefully frame my own role as the researcher as well as the role of Celie, the research participant. Through reflecting on my analysis of the online and face-to-face interactions, I show that I see Celie as an individual whose comments and experiences are her own and cannot be seen as representative of the experiences of African-American women on the campus where I conducted my research, or on other college campuses. At the same time, however, I also realized that it is important to acknowledge the long and arduous struggle for civil rights and equal rights, and the "structural silence" that, according to Michele Wallace (1993), is the outcome of Black women's oppression in political, social, and educational realms.

In Chapter 5, I look at how my interpretation of authority, and my theoretical understanding of how authority can be redistributed, became the foundation of my analysis of an online group discussion. I show that I wanted to redefine established perceptions of authority—my own and those of the students participating in the online discussion—in order to understand and change our roles in a seemingly hierarchical and authoritarian society. The online comments, however, made me realize that online environments do not always provide a setting where we can learn from each other and capitalize from a variety of ideas and opinions while at the same time moving away from autonomous toward dialogic authority. Although it seemed that some of the online exchanges provided a medium for dialogic interaction and dialogic authority, others reverted to what I consider to be authoritarian discourse patterns that did not enhance communication or immediately increase students' social awareness of the issue discussed—rape and date rape.

In Chapter 6, I move from exploring specific online interactions to an examination of how specific social, political, cultural, historical, and economic backgrounds can help, hinder, encourage, discourage, persuade, or dissuade individuals from exploring technological literacies and from participating in the so-called technology revolution. I worked with two women—Jolita and Mani—who were born and grew up on the Navajo Reservation and who recently started to explore the uses of new information technologies for educational purposes. Additionally, I show the importance of reflective practices through contextualizing Jolita's and Mani's comments within their own experiences, histories, and cultural values, and within my interpretation—based on my own background as an immigrant researcher—of these experiences, histories, and cultural values.

In the concluding chapter, I provide a brief discussion of the complexities involved in engaging in reflective case study research. I point out the need for work that moves us in new directions in our conception of what valuable and acceptable research includes. I conclude by arguing that we need to embrace alternative scholarship that prompts us to move beyond the confines of currently established and supported research. If we want to discuss the complexities and instabilities of participant and researcher identity, I point out, we need to better understand who we are as researchers, and who the participants are in our studies, how we define ourselves, and how we are defined by those who read us, work with us, and influence us.

## METHODS, METHODOLOGIES, AND MOTIVATIONS

The participants in this study were selected for a variety of reasons. When I first worked with Alba and Celie, I taught a basic writing course at the University of Illinois. Alba and Celie volunteered to participate in my study, release written documents, and talk to me after the class was finished. I also met with them several times over the next few semesters to get a sense of their progress in college. I worked with Jolita and Mani at Northern Arizona University (NAU) where I met both participants, one as a student in an introductory composition course, one as a coordinator of a technological literacy program on the Navajo reservation that had its headquarters at NAU. I met Jolita in Tuba City to conduct an interview, and I went to Kayenta to talk with Mani about her work and her technological literacy experiences. All participants agreed to have the interviews I conducted with them tape-recorded and transcribed. Furthermore, the class participants excerpted in Chapter 5 provided written approval for including their comments in this research project. I was also able to meet with Alba after I had first written Chapter 3. Her feedback on the initial draft helped me rethink how I approached literacy narratives and how I interpreted student comments in class interactions, online discussions, and interviews.

I collected information and conducted interviews with numerous other participants over the last 10 years. The participants I chose to include in this book were selected to show that my approach to conducting research and to interpreting and analyzing data has shifted from a focus on analysis to a focus on reflective practices. Initially, I conducted research with students who, although they were part of a larger university community, showed their disconnectedness in their writing, their online discussions, and their face-to-face interactions. Later on, my research started to incorporate, analyze, and interpret the larger contexts in which I and my research participants engaged in literacy practices. I also wanted to show how my growing understanding of the complexities of U.S. race relations, as well as gender and class relations, has prompted a major re-thinking in my approach to research.

As an alien and international academic who came to the United States as a graduate student in 1989, I had to learn that my skin color was more important than my nationality or my experiences. I am categorized as Caucasian, White, and Anglo, and not as Austrian, European, or even legal alien. I didn't think much about U.S. perceptions of colors or nationalities when I was a citizen of Austria. My first, not very well-planned but much-anticipated, trip to the United States—when I was 19—made me aware of the glaring class differences, but it left me mostly unaware of color differences. I was the live-in nanny/au-pair to a very wealthy family in a very wealthy neighborhood, and I was hardly encouraged to leave the house. I realized for the first time that I was many worlds (maybe galaxies) apart from the lifestyle of the upper crust, and I realized that this would not be a lifestyle to which I aspired. Because of the painful experiences during the five months in the employment of the rich, I was happy to return to my home country where the rich were the farmers up the hill who raised pigs and cows and grew alfalfa, and where my family was well-known and liked.

When I decided to return to the United States 5 years after my first attempt, I had read about the U.S. political system, the history of slavery and reconstruction, the Mexican–American War, and the annihilation of Native Americans. This time, I was no longer a nanny, but I was an international graduate student who was accepted in the English Department at the University of Illinois. My English skills had improved from my first time around, but my speech was still accented and error ridden. Although I could understand the words said by Americans, I often didn't understand the underlying meaning of these words. I also didn't understand Americans as a group. They weren't interested in internationals, and they didn't seem to care about other countries or cultures. I didn't interact with many Americans, but instead formed friendships and alliances with other internationals from countries across the world. It didn't matter much that we could only communicate in less-than-perfect English and that we came from very different political and social systems; it mattered who they were as individuals in the United States, and it mattered that they identified as other than American. We had much in common and made many generalizations: We were all unable to understand why Americans were so distant and uncaring, why they were so polite on the surface but didn't want to have anything to do with us, why they celebrated Thanksgiving, and why football was such an important part of academic institutions.

At that point in my identity development I did not see much difference among White Americans, African Americans, Latinos, Japanese Americans, or any other group that could call themselves American, whether hyphenated or not. As a legal alien who didn't even have a work permit and who didn't know whether she would be allowed in the country once her student visa expired, I considered those with an American passport, birth certificate, permanent residency card, or work permit as highly privileged. I certainly knew that race relations were volatile, especially at a campus were racial slurs appeared on hallway walls, and where student groups were clearly divided by the color of their skin. I read extensively about the histories and realities of race relations. I researched affirmative action policies. I also engaged in long philosophical international graduate student discussions about equality in the American political and social system. But in the end, the dividing line between internationals and Americans was more pronounced for me than the divisions among Americans. These divisions were largely theoretical; my own experiences were practical and didn't fit into the American cultural or social framework.

When I started my research with Alba and Celie, a Latina and an African-American woman, I chose them because of their comments and their interactions in class discussions. Most of the students in this class were African American and Latino, and only a few of them were White. To me, although I had become sensitized to race and ethnicity in the U.S. system, they were all Americans who had grown up in this country and could claim it as their own. I hardly paid attention to their color differences—which many might consider a foolish and simple-minded oversight on my part. I knew that color was a factor in their upbringing, their schooling, the choices they could make, the friends they had. Color is an inevitable attribute in this country, one that often takes precedence over other attributes. It is difficult to explain that knowing these facts wasn't enough to see color the same way that many Americans seem to see it. In some ways, I could read and discuss race relations as an academic subject, denoting the problems that faced this country. But because I didn't grow up in this country and only entered the system when I was 25, the connotations associated with these discussions were—and still are—more theoretical and less personal than they are for those being raised in this country.

I am not certain whether this is an advantage or disadvantage when discussing American students' literacy development. I also don't know how I can explain that I still perceive discussions about race relations as "less personal" than my American colleagues when I live in Arizona, a border state and a state that has borders within borders. I now interact mostly with Americans, and I have long and heated discussions—at work and at home—about politics and race relations with involuntary U.S. minorities. We talk about systemic racism and individual racism. We talk about the difficulties of talking about racism. We have disagreements about how "other" perception influences "self"-perception. We discuss how racial profiling, police brutality, and violence against border crossers leads to an internalization of negative stereotyping. We try to explain how groups within groups have become alienated from each other. We ask each other questions about our backgrounds, and we are surprised when we find out that we had similar parenting experiences and similar economic backgrounds—just on different continents. We also realize that we have very different experiences, histories, and cultural backgrounds, and that we need to ask more questions if we want to learn more about each other's histories and our placement within those histories. My colleague tells me that she would never ask a U.S. Anglo person the questions she asks me, and she tells me that she would never be asked the questions I ask her. She explains that the histories are too complicated and the assumptions about what everybody should already know are too many. From this perspective, I have an advantage because I can ask questions that a U.S. national might not be willing or might not be able to ask.

My questions are not always the most sensitive or the most productive questions I could ask. One time, I asked a young Latino who told me that he was a Mexican why he considered himself a Mexican. I asked the question out of curiosity at how nationalities are defined. I am an Austrian because I was born and raised in Austria. This young man was born and raised in the United States, and to me he was an American. My question prompted complete silence at a very rambunctious dinner table; I could only assume it was because everybody was stunned that I would ask what I considered a very straightforward question. I didn't get an answer on that day, but I wasn't thrown out of the house either. Instead, the whole family had a heated discussion about how they define themselves, why they disagree about the terms they use, how words change meaning, and how politics and history influence naming.

I know that like everybody else, I am constructed, named, and renamed constantly. I know that my identity is defined through a U.S. system of categorizing. But because I am an alien, I am not only seen as "them"—I have too many questions that "they" wouldn't have to ask—nor am I an easily defined "other"—I am too invisible until I make myself visible. I don't know what my categories would or should be in this country. I just hope that my non-U.S. background and my experiences in the United States allow me to ask questions that might not get asked otherwise. I wrote this book not because I have answers to all the questions that I constantly ask, nor do I believe that I asked all the questions I should have asked. Instead, I wrote it to show how I, as a researcher, am influenced by my international background, my understanding of the U.S. political, social, and economic system, my graduate training in a U.S. educational system, and my work as an international faculty member in a U.S. university. I show that I can't know without asking somebody what U.S. nationals know. Most importantly, I show that I am not done thinking through these complicated issues of nationality, race, culture, history, and experience. I have much to ask and much to learn.

# 2

# THEORIZING IDEOLOGIES AND PRACTICES

## PAST AND PRESENT

We don't see things as they are.
We see them as we are.
—Anais Nin (1966)

I have always carefully chosen the theoretical foundations and the concomitant ideological backdrop for my research projects, and the theories I encountered have informed me and my practices. Initially, I was intrigued by Allucquère Rosanne Stone's (1995) comments in *The War of Desire and Technology*. As she pointed out so succinctly, "theorists of gender and the body view individuals' experiences of their own bodies as socially constructed, in juxtaposition to approaches which hold that the body is ontologically present to itself and the experiences of the (always unitary) 'self' that inhabits it" (p. 92) My interpretation of Stone's postmodern approach to identity construction—and the practices in which I was engaged—led me to question what Albert Borgmann (1984), a leading philosophy of technology scholar, called an *instrumentalist position*. Computers, in other words, were seen as "value-neutral tools" (p. 10), and the user was "a toolmaker and tool user" (p. 10). Instead, I considered Christina Haas and Christine Neuwirth's comments in their 1994 article that seemed to point out that we not only use computers, but they also use us. The supposedly neutral technology was actually laden with value judgments that reflect the beliefs and ideologies of the dominant culture (i.e., the culture that creates the technology). Bertram Bruce (1993) argued similarly that "the design of any technology must be understood not simply as the construction of a physical artifact to meet a functional specification, but as a process in which relations among people are realized" (p. 15). These relations, because of a White, male-oriented computer industry, are fraught with "sexism, racism, classism, and a host of other values [which run] as rapidly as electrons through the microcircuitry of tomorrow" (Zimmerman, 1983, p. 3). Looking at computer technology as an artifact that is a recreation of dominant belief systems which reinforce the marginalization of nondominant groups by privileged groups led Selfe and Selfe (1994) to label interfaces as the "cultural maps of computer systems" (p. 485). The desktop, as they pointed out, represents modern capitalism, corporate culture, and professionalism, in its exclusion of representations from nonprofessional areas (pp. 486-487). As the comments of these scholars showed me, computer use was built on a number of expectations that reflected values ingrained in a class-, gender-, race-, and age-biased society.

In the late 1980s to mid-1990s, many of the researchers interested in working with students from diverse backgrounds wanted to find out how we can arrive at a model of electronic communication that endorses difference and ambiguity, that provides a space for all students, and that enables them to think critically about the inequalities inherent in the current political systems and social relations. It was certainly no surprise to me that groups in power positions did not see an immediate need for change; their status, as my common sense and the scholarship of feminists, race theorists, cultural studies specialists, and others told me, was determined by a continuation of the existing order. Thus, effecting change was not a priority for economically and politically privileged members of society; it was, however, of great importance to groups that did not hold positions of power.

To counter existing inequalities perpetuated and newly created in the design of the new machine, I was convinced that I needed to work against the intended homogenizing values of the new technology and that I needed to accept and validate ambiguity and difference. I was certainly not alone in this endeavor. The resistance to the status quo, as Sherry Turkle (1996) pointed out, was already happening. As she argued, the "modernist computational aesthetic" that regarded programming as linear and logical was being replaced with a different aesthetic, one that "refuses modernist resolutions and requires an openness to multiple viewpoints" (p. 198).

This adherence to multiple selves was also a focal point in Donna Haraway's (1990) often-quoted explanation of the cyborg:

> We are all chimeras, theorized and fabricated hybrids of machine and organism; in short, we are cyborgs. The cyborg is our ontology; it gives

> us our politics. The cyborg is a condensed image of both imagination and material reality, the two joined centers structuring any possibility of historical transformation. In the traditions of Western science and politics—the tradition of racist, male-dominant capitalism; the tradition of progress; the tradition of the appropriation of nature as resource for the productions of culture; the tradition of reproduction of the self from the reflections of the other—the relation between organism and machine has been a border war. (p. 191)

As an ardent follower of Haraway's ideas, I was fascinated by the eloquence and clarity with which she pointed out that neither the machine nor the organism are clearly definable entities. Instead, the "confusion of boundaries" made it increasingly difficult to achieve closure and arrive at a homogeneous and unified identity. In other words, the users were influenced by the machine, but the machine could not be seen independent of its users. This symbiosis, then, necessitated the ambiguity described by Turkle and Haraway, an ambiguity that endorsed and destabilized existing power structures.

I was, and still am, all for destabilizing existing power structures. I had no difficulty discarding modernist ideas and following a brand of postmodernism that also included my interpretation of feminist ideologies. I could easily identify with the readings that espoused that there is no stable, unchanging core since I was influenced and changed by everything I experienced and read. It was not difficult for me to see that as a researcher I brought much baggage with me from my international and school backgrounds. And I agreed with Sandra Harding (1987), who pointed out that the "beliefs and behaviors of the researcher are part of the empirical evidence for (or against) the claims advanced in the results of research" (p. 9). In order to appear "not as an invisible, anonymous voice of authority, but as a real, historical individual with concrete, specific desires and interests," and to "avoid the 'objectivist' stance that attempts to make the researcher's cultural beliefs and practices invisible while simultaneously skewering the research objects' beliefs and practices to the display board" (p. 9), Harding suggested acknowledging the underlying ideologies and the various subject positions that influence our research and that also influence the participants' perceptions of the researcher. It is certainly true that I have chosen my research topics—women and online communities, involuntary minorities' positionalities in computer-mediated environments, promotion and tenure concerns for women faculty, and so on—based on my understanding of how research can influence our thinking about how we see the word and world. My writing, in other words, reflects my own background as an

English as a Second Language (ESL) speaker, a woman from an Austrian working-class family, my often skewed perceptions of academia, and my attitudes toward technology, reality, and my position within this reality.

However, when I started to engage in ethnographic and case study research, I rarely considered my own background—which I often perceived as a deficit in my chosen career path—as an important artifact for how I would interpret the information my participants shared during interviews or observations. Reading Clifford Geertz (1973, 1988) provided a theoretical foundation for doing research. It certainly made sense to use thick description and to triangulate my data. Wendy Bishop (1992) was an easy and interesting read, and her question about "doing" research was compelling: "How could research that seemed more and more to rely on my subjectivity, interpretations, and finally, storytelling skills be a vehicle for reliable and valid results?" (p. 148). She had to realize, she argued, that researchers were never objective recorders but instead use *logos*, *pathos*, and *ethos* to arrive at their interpretation of a particular event, thus emphasizing the rhetorical nature of research methods and reports (p. 149). Other scholars—Linda Brodkey (1994), Carl Herndl (1991), Barbara Walvoord and Lucille McCarthy (1990), and Gesa Kirsch and Joy Ritchie (1995)—similarly suggested the need for "reciprocal, dialogic, collaborative, and mutually beneficial relations between researchers and participants" (Kirsch & Ritchie, 1995, p. 16).

I saw it essential in my research to follow these concepts and to incorporate them into my own approach to my studies. However, as my early work shows, I did not see myself as a participant in my research, but instead I wanted to remain the researcher whose own identity construction was acknowledged but was hardly ever fully—or even half-heartedly—explored. I did not elaborate on the connections between my own background and what I was currently researching—although I made connections in my research between a participant's early educational experiences, her gender and class backgrounds, and her perceptions of technology and college education later on in her life. My own childhood seemed very far removed—in time and distance.

Despite my reluctance to bring in my own background, as an ESL student whose command of English was not all it could be, I could easily relate to Min-Zhan Lu's (1992) comments on how teachers and researchers saw basic writers:

> The residual distrust of conflict and struggle in the field of Basic Writing is sustained by a fascination with cures for psychic woes, by two views of education—as acculturation and as accommodation—and by two

> views of language—essentialist and utopian. We need more research which critiques portrayals of Basic Writers as belonging to an abnormal—traumatized or underdeveloped mental state. (p. 910)

Like students from U.S. nontraditional backgrounds, I often considered myself an added burden to the already stressful lives of college professors and teaching assistants. The perceived "lack" of academic discourse conventions and language restrictions put me "at risk," often needing additional time and help to succeed in my courses despite my successful college work at the University of Vienna. Because of my different literacy background and my unfamiliarity with American academic discourse conventions, I was put into basic ESL courses by a well-intentioned administrator who assumed that my "cultural deficit" could be redressed by teaching me how to use articles and prepositions, and how to write a concise, well-constructed sentence. Little thought was given to the intricate reasons for the variations in literate behaviors that I brought to the university setting.

Once my accent became less audible, my cultural deficit was less visible, although it has never completely disappeared. But I paid less attention to my non-native speaking background than to my budding feminism. Anger with the world at large, and a world set against acknowledging women's equal rights provided much of the backdrop of my early feminist thinking. But it soon became clear that feminism could be very exclusive, especially when feminist scholars neglected to account for the many possible reasons for exclusion from/inclusion into a specific discourse community. After the initial euphoria of finding the secret to life's injustices, I realized that feminist research, like all research, needs to be read and applied critically; otherwise, easy assertions about the gendered nature of discourse can become the focal point of research without accounting for other, similarly important, components of interactive behavior. For example, I soon realized that the complexities of a working-class woman's struggles in a traditional male world cannot be understood only in terms of her gender, but must also be seen in terms of her status based on her educational, cultural, ethnic, social, and economic background.

Despite research that acknowledges and insists on the complexities of gender, many studies on gender differences conducted over the last three decades assumed that gender is the essential defining factor in the appropriation of rhetorical strategies. These studies portrayed language use and discourse strategies as gender-specific, but largely independent of other cultural, social, and environmental influences (see, e.g., Fishman, 1983; Henley, 1975; Penelope & Wolfe, 1983; Kramarae & Treichler, 1990; McCracken, 1992; 1983; Swacker, 1975; Zimmerman & West, 1975). The reports on those differences were widely accepted by the reading public and by those interested in gender relations and interactions. The continuing demand for *You Just Don't Understand* (Tannen, 1990) and *Men Are From Mars, Women Are From Venus* (Gray, 1992), suggests the popularity of books dealing with irreconcilable differences between men's and women's discourse conventions.

Although I was receptive to feminist ideas and strongly supported women's rights to equal pay, rights to their own bodies, or rights to equal job opportunities, I hardly saw my own concerns and ideas represented in the work of feminists who portrayed gender issues as the essential problem facing women in social interactions, at the workplace, in politics, or on the playground. Scholarship that provided a better foundation for my own research interests led me to feminist researchers who took women's social, cultural, economic, and ethnic backgrounds into consideration. I agreed with Flax (1990) who pointed out that "feminist theories . . . should encourage us to tolerate and interpret ambivalence, ambiguity, and multiplicity as well as to expose the roots of our needs for imposing order and structure no matter how arbitrary and oppressive these needs may be" (p. 56). I became especially interested in the work of scholars such as bell hooks (1981, 1984, 1989, 1992, 1994), Susan Jarratt (1991), Marsha Houston (1992), Gloria Anzaldúa (1987), and many others who had begun to acknowledge ambiguity and complexity in their work on women's issues. I was impressed by hooks' (1981) writing. Early on in her career, she emphasized the need to accept differences and to go beyond White feminists' emphasis on gender alone. To her, feminism:

> is not simply a struggle to end male chauvinism or a movement to ensure that women will have equal rights with men; it is a commitment to eradicate the ideology of domination that permeates Western Culture on various levels—sex, race, and class, to name a few--and a commitment to reorganizing U.S. society so that the self-development of people can take precedence over imperialism, economic expansion, and material desires (p. 195)

hooks also argued very convincingly that to be "feminist" in "any authentic sense of the term is to want for all people, female and male, liberation from sexist role patterns, domination, and oppression" (p. 195). She evoked the same sentiments in her 1994 work in which she stated that "I have placed alongside the struggle to end racism a commitment to ending sexism and sexist oppression, to eradicate systems of class exploitation" (p. 27). Instead of learning "obedience to authority" (p. 4), which became the primary lesson in her—as well as in my—college career, she advocated "education as the practicc of freedom" (p. 4). With these words, hooks invoked the ideas of one of my early heroes who, during my college career, changed my approach to thinking and teaching—the Brazilian educator Paulo Freire (1968, 1973) who advocated critical pedagogy to change the consciousness of those oppressed by the hierarchical structure but also of those who are in positions of power. hooks (1994) was able to use Freire's emphasis on critical awareness—action and reflection—to strengthen her own pedagogical practices that "have emerged from the mutually illuminating interplay of anticolonial, critical, and feminist pedagogies" (p. 10).

hooks' work was not the only one that pointed out to me and many others the problems with traditional feminist research. Susan Jarratt (1991), for example, in "Feminism and Composition," argued that social differences have to be a major concern in research on women's positions within society. She recounted her experience in the academy where "affirming the voice of a white, middle- or upper-middle-class student often involves teachers in rationalizing a future in corporate anonymity, in endorsing the clichés of competitive self-interest that perpetuate a system of racism, sexism, and classism still very much a part of American culture" (p. 109). Lourdes Torres (1992) expressed a similar perspective when she argued that "because gender is a category which interacts with all other categories such as age, ethnicity, race, occupation, and class, it would be useful as a point of departure from which to analyze the variation and diversity inherent in human language" (pp. 286-287).

In a more explicit critique of White feminist research, Marsha Houston (1992) admonished those who excluded feminist women from nondominant social groups from their feminist agenda. According to Houston, "discussions of theory and research about race and class differences among women are necessarily discussions of our power to construct those differences in what we say and write—to obscure and distort, or to illumine and clarify the ways in which diverse groups of women make meaning" (p. 47). She invoked Audre Lorde's words to accentuate her convictions:

> As women, we have been taught to either ignore our differences or to view them as causes for separation and suspicion, rather than as forces for change. Without community, there is no liberation, only the most vulnerable and temporary armistice between an individual and her oppression. But community must not mean a shedding of our differences, nor the pathetic pretense that these differences do not exist .("An Open Letter," p. 99, cited in Houston, 1992, p. 45)

When I worked on my research, I did not want to be one of the "communication theorists, researchers, and teachers" who "exercise considerable social power through the public discourse of our discipline" and who use that power to "conduct research in the same racist, sexist, classist, social context experienced by all other communicators" (p. 47). Such research, Houston argued, would lead to a denial of the "interlocking identities" and "interlocking oppressions" experienced by women of nondominant groups (p. 49). Instead of ignoring differences, I wanted to conduct research that would appreciate women "as enculturated to a gendered communication ideal *within* specific ethnic groups, that is, as learning how they would communicate as women in the context of a particular ethnic cultural experience" (p. 53). I agreed with Houston's appraisal that

> like the parts of nondominant women's identities, their experiences of oppression cannot accurately be conceived as separable, summative, or "piled on." For example, women of color do not experience sexism *in addition* to racism, but sexism *in the context of* racism; thus, they cannot be said to bear an *additional* burden that white women do not bear, but to bear an altogether *different* burden from that borne by white women. (p. 49)

Another scholar I admired, Gloria Anzaldúa (1987), expressed her belief in the complicated nature of inclusion–exclusion and oppressor–oppressed and argued that

> *En unas pocas centurias*, the future will belong to the mestiza. Because the future depends on the breaking down of paradigms, it depends on the straddling of two or more cultures. By creating a new mythos—that is, a change in the way we perceive reality, the way we see ourselves, the ways we behave—*la mestiza* creates a new consciousness. (p. 80)

To achieve this new "*mestiza* consciousness," Anzaldúa suggested that the mestiza needed to

> break down the subject–object duality that keeps her a prisoner and to show in the flesh and through the images in her work how duality is transcended. The answer to the problem between the white race and the colored, between males and females, lies in healing the split that originates in the very foundation of our lives, our culture, our languages, our thoughts. A massive uprooting of dualistic thinking in the individual and collective consciousness is the beginning of a long strug-

> gle, but one that could, in our best hopes, bring us to the end of rape, of violence, of war. (p. 80)

I felt comfortable that if we take the wide range of women's discourse strategies into consideration, we would be less likely to make essentializing assumptions that put women in opposition to men. Thus, looking at different strategies used by different women but also the various strategies used by the same woman in different situations could lead to more constructive interactions between the genders and among women from different backgrounds. This scholarship also showed that assumptions about essentialized gendered discourse and gendered rhetorical strategies are problematic if we want to move against believing in the passive and victimized status of women who are seen as the subject of the male gaze and the male pen. And, I was also sure that the multifaceted issues stressed by these scholars would allow us to change the focus of feminist research to stress the diversity of rhetorical acts instead of restricting our research agenda and methodologies to investigating narrowly defined and sometimes restrictive research questions.

However, continuous research and continuous discussions with colleagues and friends brought other realities to the foreground—the reality of everyday life and the reality that we will never be able to know another person's reality to its fullest extent. As a result, my writing has shifted to show a growing awareness of the many constraints that teachers and administrators face when trying to institute changes in an already established system. It is easy to write about the need for more tolerance, opportunities, and awareness of the needs of involuntary minority students; however, it is more difficult to acknowledge that change comes slowly and that many teachers, advisors, staff members, and administrators are already aware of the problems at hand but are mired in day-to-day work that does not allow them to engage in large-scale reforms that read so well on paper.

Furthermore, realizing that I cannot know anybody else's reality—or that I cannot and do not want to achieve what Iris Marion Young (1997) called "symmetrical reciprocity"—encouraged me to take a critical look at previous assumptions about how I can and want to interpret participants' words and actions. I found Young's argument that we cannot put ourselves in other people's places especially compelling after being convinced for years that viable research could only be conducted if I could claim that I knew as well as understood my participants and could therefore draw the right conclusions in my research. Young's work on asymmetrical reciprocity helped me understand that I could only respect my participants if I did not assume knowledge about the other that I could never achieve. Young used three arguments to make a case against symmetrical reciprocity. As she so succinctly put it:

> first, this idea of a symmetry in our relation obscures the difference and particularity of the other position. Second, it is ontologically impossible for people in one social position to adopt the perspective of those in the social positions with which they are related in social structures and interaction. The idea that moral respect involves taking the other people's point of view, finally, can have politically undesirable consequences. (p. 44)

Young suggested, based on her reading of Emmanuel Levinas and Luce Irigaray, that we need to understand reciprocity as mutual respect and acknowledgment of each other. She quoted Nancy Love who argued that "Individuals cannot 'stand inside' another's world and adopt their 'world-view,' nor should they try to do so. However, they can communicate across the distance and their differences. Voice crosses, even while it respects, boundaries" (p. 50).

It is easy to understand and grasp the concept of asymmetrical reciprocity explored by Iris Marion Young. What is more difficult, however, is to put into practice the concepts addressed by Young. I want to believe that I don't attempt to put myself into other people's shoes, understanding the futility of such an approach. But, when I point out that "I know exactly what you mean," or when I write that "I can relate to where my students are coming from," I assume an unwarranted symmetrical reciprocity that is impossible to achieve. Do I, however, understand their point of view without conflating it with my own? Do I "wonder" enough to appreciate the different perspectives of others without exoticizing them? Can I admit that I don't know what it means to be disabled? To show respect for others, and to "make our moral and political judgments," Young suggested taking into account "one another's interests and perspectives" and considering "the collective social processes and relationships that lie between us and which we have come to know together by discussing the world" (p. 59).

To show that I respected my participants and that I took their perspectives into consideration, I thought it especially important to give full voice to them. I wanted to make sure their comments would be heard, and that my interpretation of their comments would take a back seat. Leaving information out, I was convinced, would not give full credit to my participants' literacy stories, and it would also render them partly voiceless. I was relying on feminist approaches to research, acknowledging that "feminist inquiry joins other 'underclass' approaches in insisting on the importance of studying ourselves and 'studying up,' instead of 'studying down'" (Harding, 1987, p. 8). I listened for many hours to my participants; however, I am now doubtful that my early research incorporated Young's convincing call for dialogue in order to understand others. Her explanation of asymmetrical reciprocity provided me with a starting point to pay more attention to how I construct my and my research participants' identities. According to Young, asymmetrical reciprocity means that

> We meet and communicate. We mutually recognize one another and aim to understand one another. Each is open to such understanding by recognizing our asymmetry. A condition of our communication is that we acknowledge the difference, interval, that others drag behind them shadows and histories, scars and traces, that do not become present in our communication. Thus we each must be open to learning about the other person's perspective, since we cannot take the other person's standpoint and imagine that perspective as our own. (p. 53)

I have become more conscious of my participants' and my own stated and unstated positionalities when I conduct research. I try to provide as much thick description and triangulation as I possibly can, and I pay close attention to Bishop's as well as Kirsch and Ritchie's commentary on ethics in research, and I am strongly supportive of Katrina Powell and Pamela Takayoshi's (2003) argument for reciprocity in research. But I also know that I cannot deny my own affiliations and affinities, nor can I always assume that my research is beneficial to my participants. Certainly, I have read and also written about making research more transparent, and incorporating the researcher into the research; however, many of these attempts at providing information about the researcher, although telling us who she or he is, fall short of providing a critical examination of a researcher's underlying, often hidden, and always changing goals and perspectives. Furthermore, the "shadows and histories" addressed by Young are an additional reason for being vigilant about how we approach and conduct research.

For this reason, I was impressed with Min-Zhan Lu's 1999 lecture on "Redefining the Literate Self: The Politics of Critical Affirmation," in which she discussed how her own predilections and ideologies influence her reading and writing. Her call for "critical affirmation" and her sketches of four abuses of identity politics helped my own thinking about how to incorporate the personal into my research.

I would like to argue that I don't write the personal for capital investment, that I don't use the personal as a mirror reflection of a self or culture, that I don't slot myself or others as being able to speak for a group, and that I don't disembody the personal (see Lu, 1999, pp. 1-3). But it is also important to acknowledge that personal narrative—or self-reflexivity—can become "self-indulgent or narcissistic" (Powell & Takayoshi, 2003, p. 155). In other words, despite conscious efforts not to use identity politics for individual gain, it is often difficult to escape the unconscious or subconscious tendencies to justify, defend, and promote an individual, albeit theoretically founded and supported, perspective. Why, for example, do I discuss my international status in some of my writing? Do I assume that this provides me with immunity against attack, being able to claim ignorance of some of the finer points of U.S. gender, race, and class politics? Or do I bring in my international perspective to show that my experiences can shed new light on old fights, a light that no U.S. citizen was able to shed? Either way, I am speaking in "particular ways" and might appear "trendy and thus trite" (Lu, 1999, p. 2), or worse, an intellectual snob.

And, do I remember that "the self is an on-going, complex, conflicted, and transformative process" (Lu, 1999, p. 2) when I incorporate the personal in my writing, or do I see my narrative as exempt from the scrutiny I apply to the writings of other scholars? I certainly know that lived experience is not static and has to be approached as a continuously changing process. Sometimes, however, despite my best intentions, it is difficult to underscore the discursive nature of my experiences and to take into account the complexities of personal stories. I often remind myself that I create my own history by writing the personal. I emphasize certain aspects of my life and gloss over others. Much of my own history is also lost because my recollection of events is spotty or nonexistent. Other parts of my histories are not my own recollections but those of my family or friends. In other words, we live through stories, or we are told stories about ourselves, and we interpret them according to our own interpretations of what the events meant to us. As Lu said, I need to be more conscious about exploring my experiences through "the mediation of a complex network of power, desire, and interests" (p. 3) instead of seeing them as "a self-evident thing existing prior to and outside of discursive practices" (p. 3).

Furthermore, do I remind myself often enough that I cannot make easy assumptions about individuals or even about myself? If I agree that my and others' experiences are mediated through a vast array of tangible and intangible signifiers, it is highly improbable that I will be able to attach a specific and unalterable motive to my own actions and the actions of other individuals who I work with as participants in my research, or who I read as sources of inspiration, confirmation, or critique. For example, reading Lu's piece provides a wonderful contextualization on why I should be more aware of the importance of critical affirmation. It also shows Lu's thinking about research and about taking responsibility for previously published research. But reading her article does not give me license to make assumptions about Lu's political, historical, economic, or gender background beyond the stories revealed by Lu herself. It is also important to remind myself that my interpretation of her writing and her comments on growing up outside the United States is influenced by my own experiences as an international faculty member. Conversely, however, my international status should not give me license to represent others who did not grow up in this country and who have experienced a variety of struggles and challenges. My lens is the lens of the academic who has been modestly successful in her profession. It is not the lens of the immigrant who struggles to make ends meet, or the lens of the immigrant who has become a national and international icon for bodybuilding success, international movie blockbusters, and political ingenuity.

And, finally, how do I represent myself and my research participants in my writing? Do I want to fit them "neatly within simplistic notions of race, sex, class, and gender" (p. 3) or do I allow for more complex representations of self and other in my research? How do I present concepts and ideas that don't lend themselves to easy explanations? I, like many other scholars and teachers, have emphasized the postmodern, feminist, and cyborgian flexibilities when I discuss mine and my participants' realities and identities; however, it is easy to arrive at an interpretation that is final and restrictive, conforming to our perceptions of how the actions and words of specific groups and people need to fit into a predictable pattern. In other words, if a Native American student does poorly on a quiz, it is often assumed that this student cannot relate to linear ways of thinking or is going through culture shock. But, do we consider the multiplicities of reasons for poor performance? Did the student study for the quiz? Does the student have another test that's more important? Did the student have to attend to a family emergency? Did the student have access to the book? In other words, my research needs to consider whether to attribute a student's failure in school solely to cultural differences or to other, often equally important reasons. Thus, instead of making easy assumptions—this student is Native American, therefore there must be a cultural reason for his or her difficulties—it is important that I ask questions that let me see a student's or research participant's reality from a wide range of perspectives, and that lets me make connections that are not always popular or expected. Of course, little research has been done on these connections, and Lu's research has prompted me to attend more carefully to what Lu, in referring to Richard Miller's work, called "the social construction of our private, visceral reactions when reading and writing" (p. 3).

I have learned much from recent research by Nancy Barron, who, in her 2003 article, "Dear Saints, Dear Stella: Letters Examining the Messy Lines of Expectations, Stereotypes, and Identity in Higher Education," used a letter format to discuss how Latino students are perceived by the Anglo mainstream and how Latino students perceive the Anglo mainstream. Barron's work is grounded in accepted theoretical frameworks; however, what is most absorbing and refreshing about Barron's approach is her focus on the particular and her insistence that race, gender, and class cannot be abstracted for the sake of easy conclusions. Her struggle to discuss the complexities of her own experiences as well as the complex experiences of Latinos in academic settings is an excellent example of Lu's insistence on paying attention to the diverse voices of those we research, to our own intuitions, and to how these intuitions are influenced by the identities we construct for ourselves and for others. As Barron pointed out in her work, "we all come together with constructions of one another. The problem is we often have the wrong constructions, and we use filters that inevitably will cancel out the other's intentions, good or bad" (p. 32). I found it helpful to read Barron's argument for keeping open to difference. As she puts it, "I seem to work best with those academics who don't pretend to know me, who don't pretend to understand diversity, who don't pretend they know how they're perceived, and who are curious and genuinely allow for change in their own thinking and ways of doing things" (p. 17). Like Young (1997), Barron very succinctly pointed out the need to listen without judging and without assuming knowledge. This is especially important when we work with students whose cultural, religious, social, and educational backgrounds are very different from our own. For example, I recently read in *The Nation* magazine that 40% of Americans are born-again Christians (Press, 2004). My vivid imagination automatically jumps to stereotypes of conservative Christians that might or might not be true. As *The Nation* writer pointed out, born-again Christians come from various backgrounds, have various political affiliations, and support a variety of social and political viewpoints. My preconceived notions would not have allowed such diversity, but instead, I would have "pretended to know" where born-agains were coming from—and where they were going.

## HISTORIES, STORIES, TECHNOLOGIES

I had to learn—and am still learning—to contextualize not only the worlds in which my students, colleagues, and research participants live, but also the worlds that have influenced my own literacy experiences, the professional choices I make and made, and the theories I have about the histories, politics, and cultures I experience on a daily basis. Although women academics have been reluctant in the past to discuss their backgrounds, we now can read stories and narratives of socialization published in various journals and in book-length form. Min Zhan Lu (2001), for example, pointed out in *College English* that "to break down the polarities dictating our understanding of our lives in relation to the people, history, culture, and institutions around us," we need "to move our thinking beyond a mere fixation on the 'what's' of the lived experience to also explore the 'how's' and 'why's to our lived experience" (p. 53). In her memoir, where she provided insights into her life in a Catholic Chinese family, the Cultural Revolution, the move to the United States, and her life in a new world, she also reaffirmed the need for self-reflection. Furthermore, a recent *College English* special issue (2003) on creative nonfiction emphasized the increasing importance of personal writing in composition scholarship.

One of the early essays in the field of composition studies that showed me the importance of incorporating the self into the research we take on was Linda Brodkey's (1994) exploration of her own background in "Writing on the Bias." Here, she related her experiences as a working-class girl who was tracked for college. She is aware that "the educational opportunities that thrilled [her] contradicted most of what was expected at home" (p. 543). She described the economic struggles her parents went through in order to allow her to go to college, but also highlighted the emotional support she received from them. Her emphasis on her family, especially her mother's sewing while Brodkey was writing, situates her story within a strong allegiance to her family. Similarly, Lilian Bridwell-Bowles (1995) discussed how she tried to accommodate the various literacies from her "multiple worlds." She posed the following question to the readers:

> So what does it mean to write or to learn to write from multiple perspectives? From a personal perspective, my life has been directly touched by racism, by war, by AIDS, and by the feminist movement. As I have been touched, I have changed and my language and my rhetoric have changed. (p. 55)

Bridwell-Bowles concluded her essay by pointing out that "I have attempted to place [my pedagogical practices] within the dialectic of identity politics and society's aim for education" (p. 60).

Because my identity is mediated by other people, by the media, and by texts I read, and because I mediate what will be presented in the texts

I write, I do not assume that I write without bias or that I don't have preconceived notions about the world around me. To use Gunther Kress' (2003) words, "knowing, as experience, the effects of culture—feeling it in my body even now in the move, say, from one language to another, from one style of writing to another—has given my academic work its shape and purpose: trying to understand how we as humans come to be who we are in our cultural and social environments" (pp. 13-14). My designation as a legal alien in the United States has introduced me to some of the challenges of living and working in a culture that is not my own. The history of my country is very distinct from that of the United States. Hundreds of years of monarchy, feudal lords, and empire building were replaced in 1918 with a fledgling democracy. Twenty years later, Austria became part of the Third Reich, and World War II left many scars, destroyed homes, severed families, and killed millions of innocent people. But 7 million people decided to rebuild my country in the 1940s and 1950s with the help of neighbors, friends, and family. Instead of an empire where the sun never sets, Austria is now a tiny speck that people know because of an Austrian-born California governor, and because of an American-produced musical, *The Sound of Music*, which very nicely portrays many of the stereotypes I have heard about my country.

My own history is part of this larger picture. The stories my grandparents and parents tell are intertwined with the war experiences they have had. My grandfather has talked about escaping from a Russian prison camp in World War I; my parents have told stories about hiding escaped World War II prisoners of war in barrels and haystacks, fighting off the sexual advances of the occupying forces who stayed after World War II to protect my country, trying to smuggle food across the four dividing lines occupied by British, French, American, and Russian forces for 10 years after the war ended, and hoping that they would leave soon.

For many years, these stories were part of my growing up, and for many years, my perceptions of the war and the people who fought it were influenced more by the stories I heard than by the books I read. I still relate to these stories more than I relate to the sanitized versions that my teachers presented. And although I didn't experience the war years, I am influenced by them, and I look at other events through the lens of my parents' war stories. When I read and talk about slavery, when I hear about the problems in inner-city schools, when I listen to stories about Native-American displacements, and when I write about the experiences of my research participants, I use my own framework to relate to these events, a framework that's not just academic but that has its roots in the stories that I heard, and that changes with the stories I am still hearing. I decide on the "*kinds* of research" (Kirsch, 1993, p. 55) partly because of the experiences I have had and still have.

When I teach, or when I conduct research, I also think about my parents' stories, about their school experiences, and about my own struggle to figure out what I wanted to do. My father hated school, with a passion, and he was very vocal about the many hours he wasted in a classroom studying English when he could have done something more productive and useful, such as fixing another plow or shoeing another horse. My mother, on the other hand, wanted to become a school teacher, but her family couldn't afford to send their daughter to school. They needed her to help at home with the other kids, and they also needed her to work for the farmer to pay for their strip of land. Instead of teaching at school, my mother taught six kids how to value who we are and what we achieved. I learned very early on that education does not only happen in school, but that there are many ways of being educated and being literate.

Becoming literate in computer technologies at a relatively late stage in my life was one of my most painful school-literacy experiences. Because typing was not my strong subject in school, and because my teacher told me I would never succeed in any job that required typing skills, I avoided computers for many years. They were glorified typewriters that reminded me too much of the teacher who almost failed me when I didn't type enough words per minute on my typewriting exams. Finally, one of my ESL instructors in the United States forced all his students to use computers. Sitting in a big, sterile lab, not knowing what keys to press or where to put the disk, was a humbling if not humiliating experience. It took me many months to understand the basic functions of a computer. It became a simple tool—we typed our papers, and we practiced grammar rules. It didn't occur to me until later that I could theorize my computer experiences. I can now say that I saw technology as neutral (Borgman, 1984), as a tool that allowed me to hand in papers that looked neat and clean and that would hopefully improve my grammar skills. I didn't question the various uses and abuses of technology. My critical awareness was only raised in my last year of my master's program, when I was asked to teach first-year composition in a computer lab and when I started to take courses in rhetoric and composition. It was an eye-opening experience, and I quickly learned about Albert Borgmann's (1984) four-part theory of technology, Andrew Feenberg's (1991) attempts to provide a critical theory of technology, Haraway's (1990) cyborg, Carol Stabile's (1994) discussions of feminism and technology, and Allucquere Rosanne Stone's (1995) explorations of technology's position at the end of the mechanical age. I have learned much from my experiences and my readings, and I am continuously learning more. With every discussion, every interaction, every new reading, I find that I need to revise and rethink my assumptions and my approaches to technological literacy. Stuart Selber (2004), for example, pushed me to think differently about functional, critical, and rhetorical technological literacy, encouraging me to work with students on becoming reflective producers of technology. Similarly, when I consider the work of Cynthia Selfe and Gail Hawisher (2000, 2004), I know that I need to learn more about the social, political, historical, cultural, and economic environments in which I, my colleagues, and my students practice technological literacy.

As my mother used to say when my efforts in cooking, sewing, or writing neatly once again failed, "Nothing is ever simple. Just try it again." These words still guide my research and my teaching, and they have encouraged me to try again and to look carefully at the multifaceted nature of technology and how technology influences political, economic, social, cultural, and gender issues. Similar to Jane Hindman (2001), I have realized that "embodied writing and reading require me to surrender my analytical need to be right and/or absolute in my understanding of how language [literacy acquisition, history, politics, gender] works" (p. 101). I also know, that like Hindman, I need to engage in "unflinching self-reflection, maintaining a relentless awareness of the ways I use rhetoric to position myself" (p. 101).

The following chapters are an attempt to place my interpretation and analysis of my research participants' comments and uses of technology within such a self-reflective framework. I hope to show that as researchers we need to highlight that our own literacies, our ideologies, and our predilections are integral to how we approach and conduct research, and how we choose, analyze, and compose the stories that our research participants share with us.

# 3

# LIVING IN DIFFERENT CULTURES

## EXPERIENCES OF THE BORDERLANDS

When I considered different titles for this chapter, I wanted to make sure that readers would approach Alba's story as the story of someone whose identities were formed by the different cultures that were part of her life. With the reference to Anzaldúa's (1987) work *Borderlands/La Frontera*, I wanted to show from the beginning that Alba's worlds are the worlds of somebody on the fringes, somebody who doesn't fit nicely into pre-set categories. It is a conscious choice that is intended to predispose readers in a specific way. I want them to see Alba as somebody who is not mainstream, who cannot assume that her home and school environments are closely related, and who might encounter difficulties based on her cultural and ethnic backgrounds.

At the same time, the title of the chapter foregrounds how I analyzed Alba's comments and interactions. I chose a specific lens mainly informed by scholarship on race and ethnicity, gender studies, and basic writing research. My interest in identity politics is evident in my interpretations of how Alba's background influences her comments and interactions online. As Powell and Takayoshi (2003) pointed out so well, my findings, and my analysis of Alba's online interactions—as well as the interactions of all participants in this study—are "directly influenced by who [I am], what [I know], and what decisions [I] make at the research site" (p. 154).

What I want to show in this chapter is twofold. I want to show the complicated positionalities that Alba occupies at the university, in the classroom, and in her home environment. I also want to show that as a researcher I need to be critically aware of my own interpretations of my work and my own positionalities as the researcher and teacher in this context. Here, I reflect on the personal to make clear my positions, not to put Alba "neatly within simplistic notions of race, sex, class, and gender" (Lu, 1999, p. 3), but to provide a framework for reading Alba's comments and for reading my interpretation and analysis of her comments. It is the process of arriving at conclusions that is foregrounded in this chapter more so than the conclusions themselves. Like all researchers, I could draw many different conclusions, depending on what I emphasize and what lenses I use to conduct my research and my analysis. In a sense, this chapter could be considered as blurring autobiography and ethnography which, according to William Tierney (1998) "confronts dominant forms of representation and power in an attempt to reclaim, through self-reflexive response, representational spaces that have marginalized those of us on the borders" (p. 66, quoting Neumann, 1996, p. 189). The role of the author in this situation, according to Tierney, "is to help provide definition and scope to individuals, so that readers are able to locate the text within larger representational practices" (p. 66). This approach, as Deborah Reed-Danahay (1997) argued, "reflects a changing conception of both the self and society" (p. 2). In other words, by reinterpreting how we see ourselves and the communities around us, we also need to reinterpret how we do research and how we talk about our research.

I am convinced that no research can ever be complete and can address all the questions that a researcher wants to address or that readers might want to see addressed. But I am also convinced that it is the responsibility of the researcher to provide the reader, through self-reflexive practices, insights into the researcher's ideological framework, theoretical foundations, and textual analyses. Here, then, my story is interwoven with Alba's to show how my own background influenced my reading of Alba's story and my subsequent interpretation of Alba's online comments.

## OBSERVING ALBA

When I talked with Alba, a first-year Latina student enrolled in a basic writing class at a major midwestern university almost 10 years ago, and when I first started to write about her experiences as an involuntary minority student in a very mainstream university, I used my training in feminist studies, basic writing, and computers and writing as a lens to explore her experiences, comments, and efforts to make it through school successfully. I was hoping to find out whether Alba was placed into a basic writing course because she had not yet acquired the "cultural capital" that Bourdieu (1984) and Giroux (1992) see as part of an environment that upholds traditional Anglo, middle-class values and beliefs. Furthermore, with my research I wanted to contribute to a growing body of scholarship that explores how a computer-supported pedagogy may affect women from involuntary minority backgrounds who experience multiple barriers in an environment that privileges White middle-class discourse. Furthermore, by exploring Alba's experiences in and outside an educational setting, I wanted to show, similar to Hourigan (1994), that "basic writers differ from college to college and may even differ from year to year within a single college or university" (p. 36). And, in addition, I wanted to show that basic writers also differ from each other, making it problematic to talk about essential characteristics of these students without acknowledging the diversity among them.

My familiarity with research on basic writers was responsible for some initial assumptions about Alba about which I probably should have been more careful. Initially, I saw her through Patricia Bizzell's (1986) eyes. Bizzell observed that a common trait of basic writers is that they are "most alien in the college community" (p. 294). She attributed the difficulties experienced by "basic writers" to "differences in dialects, discourse conventions, and ways of thinking" (p. 296), all of which amount to a clash between those students' worldviews and the academic worldview (p. 297). This description seemed to fit Alba just perfectly.

One of the first comments that Alba made during an interview we conducted struck me as indicative of the concerns that students with a working-class background seem to have: "It's really sheltered down here [at the university]; you see how other people, like the middle class, live, and I see the differences if I ask somebody on their background; they'll tell me, well, you know, they already had exposure to computers and I didn't, I didn't in school." Alba did not see herself as fitting the picture of the average college student; instead, as a woman who grew up in a neighborhood that was far removed from the world known to most college students, she brought to the university all the attributes of what Bizzell (1986) termed "'outlandishness'—their appearance to many teachers and to themselves as the students who are most alien in the college community" (p. 294). Also, Alba's economic and social status—Alba ranked herself as "underclass" based on her money constraints, her neighborhood, and her lifetime experiences—reinforced her classification as "other" by the academic community.

David Bartholomae's (1985/1988) ideas in "Inventing the University" also guided me in interpreting Alba's concerns about school. Bartholomae stated that "the inexperienced writer is left with a more fragmentary record of the comings and goings of academic discourse [than the experienced writer]" (p. 284). What these students need to learn, he argued, is to "extend themselves into the commonplaces, set phrases, rituals, gestures, habits of mind, tricks of the 'what might be said' and constitute knowledge within the various branches of our academic community" (p. 278).

What follows, then, is the story that Alba shared with me during interviews, and with her classmates in online discussions. It is a story that I contextualized according to my own stories and the stories of my family. I show how I interpreted Alba's background and how I saw her interactions in an online discussion forum connected to her gender, ethnic, and racial background, and her economic situation. My intent was to look at the situated and multilayered nature of discourse created by the intersection of gender, ethnicity, race, class, and cultural and social backgrounds of the participants.

By telling Alba's story, I thought I would be able to answer the questions that Patricia Bizzell (1986) posed: "What world views do basic writers bring to college? What is the new world view demanded in college? And do basic writers have to give up the world views they bring to college in order to learn the new world-view?" (p. 297). Certainly, I did not want to forget Lu's admonition that Alba's identity would be transformed and changed by the interactions and events in her life, but I also would have liked to present definitive answers to Bizzell's questions.

## A NONTRADITIONAL WOMAN'S COMING OF AGE

When I worked with Alba, I was familiar with the work of such scholars as Gloria Anzaldúa (1987), Marsha Houston (1992), bell hooks (1994), Min-Zhan Lu (1992, 1994), and others. Their comments on the ambiguity and complexity of interpreting women's struggles in an oppressive environment guided my own theoretical framework for approaching Alba's comments and writings. After various discussions with Alba, and after reading over her responses in the online discussion forum, I was certain that Gloria Anzaldúa (1987) had Alba in mind when she described life in the borderlands:

> To live in the Borderlands means you
> are neither *hispana india negra espanola*
> *ni gabacha, eres mestiza, mulata*, half-breed
> caught in the crossfire between camps
> while carrying all five races on your back
> not knowing which side to turn to, run from. (p. 194)

Alba's story made me realize how little I knew about the students at the university, and how much I took for granted as a researcher and teacher.

I did not acknowledge until many years later that Anzaldúa's concept of the borderlands had captured my attention for very specific reasons. I was not overly familiar with the border politics between Mexico and the United States, but I had to figure out border crossing ever since I decided to leave home for the United States. It meant to cross a physical border, but it also meant to change attitudes, mindsets, behaviors, clothing, and food preferences. I certainly did not encounter the racist stereotypes that were associated with being "Mexican" in a prejudiced country. My accent was not very heavy, and I could pass for a mainstream American if I wanted to. But I couldn't really be an American, nor did I want to be acculturated when I had so many concerns and insecurities about my status as an alien—not alien enough to make it on Mr. Spock's TV series, but alien enough to worry about crossing borders.

I interpreted Alba's story about her mother, who grew up in the United States, and her grandfather, who was from Nicaragua, based on my own experiences as an immigrant. According to the stories that Alba heard, her grandfather had a hard childhood. He was orphaned early on in his life and made it all the way to the United States when he was 8 years old. What that really meant is a mystery to Alba, but she heard many times how affectionately her mother talked about her grandfather. He made it to the United States, and he was able to buy gifts for his children and to take them everywhere in the United States because he believed that his children deserved to have everything that he didn't have. He treated Alba's grandmother like a queen and valued his family because, as Alba was told, he didn't have one himself when he grew up. Alba didn't hear much in school about Nicaragua, immigration policies, or the conflicts between the United States and the Nicaraguan government. She knew these stories because her grandfather lived through them and talked about them with his family.

Similar to Alba, I was interested in the stories my own grandfather told. But in this case it wasn't about leaving one's home for a better place, but about the monarchy and World War I. He told stories about the last Austrian emperor, Franz Josef, who died during World War I but who lived on in his memories as the great ruler of a divided country. He also told us about his own experiences during the war, the atrocities that were carried out, and of his time in an internment camp in Russia. My parents talked about World War II and its aftermath, the teachers who resisted Nazi ideology and disappeared, the fear that parents would be taken away and older sisters molested. In school, we learned about the peace treaty and Austria's surprising recovery and survival as a free and independent nation. The dates that we had to memorize, however, were much less meaningful than the stories I heard at home.

When Alba's mother married a Mexican national at a fairly young age, Alba says her mother was "caught between two worlds," partly because she wanted to live in the United States but her husband wanted to go back to Mexico. The job situation was unstable and did not bring the expected monetary relief. Another reason for the difficulties in her mother's life was her husband's attitudes toward women. Alba's father came to the United States in his 20s and, according to Alba, had a "different" childhood and a "different" view toward life. Alba explains that her grandfather used to beat his wife, and that her father picked up the habit and beat her mother as well. And her grandfather did not believe in education, but instead needed his eldest son to help in the fields. Alba doesn't blame her father for his domineering behavior but only mentions that he needed to be a "macho man" to please his own father.

Alba's mother made some concessions and went to Mexico for a short period, during which Alba was born. However, the different lifestyle and the unrealistic expectations imposed on her by her husband's family brought them back to the United States, and for 14 years, the family lived in Chicago. Her mother worked as a teacher's aide and school clerk, her father as a steelworker, a job from which he often got laid off. The pressures of his sporadic unemployment, in connection with different attitudes toward monetary issues—her father took her mother's paycheck and sent it back to Mexico instead of using it for their own needs—finally resulted in divorce. Alba's father returned to Mexico; her mother stayed in the United States because, as Alba put it, "she wanted us to get an education and she knew we'd be like illiterates, illiterate farmhands in Mexico." However, before Alba's father left, he took her two younger brothers with him to Mexico without telling her mother. Alba says, he "kidnapped them, 'cause my mom wanted all of us. I guess he wanted to get back at her, so he took the two younger ones." But Alba's mother was not easily discouraged, and when Alba was 12, her mother brought her and her oldest son to Mexico. Alba's grandparents only agreed to let her younger brothers return to the United States if she left Alba and her brothers in Mexico.

Alba's mother left them, but promised to come back for them at the end of the summer.

In the meantime, Alba's father had gotten married and his wife lived with his parents, working on the farm. He was not around at the time of the incident, but was working in California and had not been to Mexico in 6 months. Alba's mother kept her promise and came back for Alba and her brothers. One of her brothers wanted to stay in Mexico, but the others returned to the United States where they moved into a two-bedroom apartment in a midwestern city, also taking in Alba's maternal grandmother. After about 8 years in Mexico, Alba's father and her younger brother, moved back to the United States. Alba saw them from time to time but had no close ties to her father.

When Alba told me this story, I thought about my father's strong opposition to my excursions into the new world. When I told him, at age 18, that I had booked a ticket to fly to Chicago, he wouldn't talk to me for days. He told my mother that he would not allow me to go, and it took several weeks of coaxing by her to make him change his mind. My mother argued that I would be staying with her brother who had come to the United States after World War II, and from what we knew, he had done very well for himself. My uncle had promised to help me find a job as a nanny. I worked for a very wealthy family with two young children and learned many of my language skills by helping them with their homework.

After the initial excitement of working in the United States, I could not fathom being a nanny for long, and I decided to go back home and find a job as a kindergarten teacher or aide. My aspirations were not very high because I had largely negative educational experiences. But my brother suggested that it would not hurt to check out the University of Vienna and take some courses until I found a job. I had never set foot in any university; I was afraid that everybody would see me for what I was: an imposter who did not even have the grades to back her up. I made sure that my brother came with me for moral support when I first registered for courses. I could not count on economic support for my studies; instead, most of my family, except for my mother, saw college as an escape from reality—work—and I was considered to be too intellectual and too far removed from what really mattered, such as earning a living and establishing a family. I had to listen to a number of questions that expressed the feelings of my family: "What do you need that for?" "What good is that going to do anybody?" "You should *do* something instead, not just read books." "Why study, it's a waste of money?" But, with a stipend from the government, I started my degree process in history and English, taking lectures and seminars, disliking some of them but liking most of them. I studied hard, and tried to get over my fear of speaking up. And instead of looking for a full-time job, I continued my degree program.

Alba's mother's insistence on a good education seemed to be one of the major reasons for Alba's positive attitude toward school. Alba attended bilingual education classes for the first 2 years, but, as she points out, "Mom really was against it, because a lot of it is tracking, so she knew that they wanted to put us in bilingual education forever." Thus, instead of staying in bilingual education, Alba was switched to regular classes and attended high school with a population of mainly African Americans (65%) and Latinos (25%–30%). During her senior year she applied to a major midwestern university and was accepted. She was a first-generation college student, which she said was a "big deal" with her family.

Of course, Alba's move away from home and her intentions to attend college caused a wide array of reactions within her family. Her grandmother was not too enthusiastic about the decision because she didn't think that Alba was serious about college. Her grandmother thought it more important for Alba to earn her own money, learn how to cook and then get married after a while. But her grandmother's misgivings were counterbalanced by her mother's support and her wish for a "better life" for her children. Alba's mother wanted her children to get a college degree because she didn't want them to take orders from somebody, but instead be able to give the orders. Her mother was convinced that she "could have done better" if she had gone to college herself. Alba did go to college, and she also wanted to go to medical school and be the first doctor in her family which, as she says, "is real big, real big."

Alba saw her move from her home environment to a college campus as a challenge because she did not think she would fit in. She designated herself as "underclass" based on her mother's low income. She saw her underclass status as having an impact on her status at the university. On this campus, she pointed out, "we are not catered to"; instead, it is middle-class students who get more attention. None of the people she grew up with and went to school with went to college with her. And, the university she went to had a much lower number of Latino students than the high school she attended.

Alba's feelings of exclusion have been shared by others coming to the university from lower economic income levels. I recalled Rose's (1989) and Rodriguez's (1981) struggles to come to terms with the difficulties they experienced as students with a working-class background. bell hooks' (1994) lower class background also had an impact on her life: She felt out of place in an environment that was not geared toward lower class students, and in her case, toward Latino students.

But Alba's feelings of exclusion were not only class based. Similar to hooks, Alba seemed to face additional challenges. Not only was her economic and social background different from those of the majority of students at the university, but her ethnic background and her position as a first-generation female college attendee were also part of her "outlandish" status. The effects of these influences made it difficult for Alba to adjust to the university and to see any similarities between her life at home and her life in school. Yet, unlike Rodriguez, who tried to assimilate middle-class values at the expense of his cultural heritage, Alba took a different position. Instead of accepting the sheltered life of a college campus and forgetting the world outside of it, Alba knew that when she returned home, she would not be able to go out after 9 P.M. or walk alone. She would meet up with her friends, many of whom had children at a young age, were members of gangs, had been in jail, and used drugs. She also knew that she had to perform according to the standards set by a white middle-class society if she wanted to fulfill her dream of going to medical school.

Alba's status at the university and her wish to continue her education after finishing her bachelor's degree, reminded me of my own hopes for graduate school. After 3 years at the University of Vienna, I applied for and received a Fulbright Scholarship to study abroad in the United States for a year. The experience was refreshing, and the new perspectives on historical events and literary currents strengthened my desire to continue graduate work. When I took my ESL classes, I got to know many of the international students who also were not considered proficient English speakers. We were not only introduced to writing papers using correct grammar, style, and formatting, but we also learned what group work meant, how to participate in discussions, and what an "honors system" was. I still felt like a fish out of water when I sat in my history class, but I knew not to take out my notes—which every student in Austria would have done—when the instructor left the room during an exam.

I was lucky to find a group of internationals when I studied at the University of Illinois. We met at least once a week, and we commiserated about the difficulties we had encountered during the week. We were a small group with members from countries all over the world. But we shared a common culture: the international student culture where nobody quite fit in, and where everybody felt outside the norm.

Although my family has problems relating to what I do and never quite understood what I studied, they have slowly become used to the idea that I have a job as a teacher at a university. My mother, although mystified when I tell her "*dass ich Englisch unterrichte*" and not *Deutsch*—which would make much more sense to anybody I know—proudly announces to her friends, neighbors, sisters, and brothers that her daughter "*ist eine Englischlehrerin in Amerika.*" And when I am visiting, she inevitably reminds me how much I hated English as a student and how sure I was that I would never set foot in an educational institution after my experiences with high school.

It was interesting to read Richard Rodriguez's (1981) account of his education and life experiences in *Hunger of Memory*. When he pointed out that "schooling was changing me and separating me from the life I had enjoyed before becoming a student" (p. 45), I thought about my move to the United States and my inability to talk to my family about my studies. It wasn't that they weren't interested or that I didn't want to let them know, but I didn't have the language to share my excitement about the projects I was working on. I studied in English, and I talked to my family in German.

I found Anzaldúa (1987) helpful in interpreting my own difficulties in communicating with my family and in understanding how Alba thought of school and home. It wasn't a matter of thinking about two or more races, or male–female dichotomies, but it was about communicating in two different worlds, whether these worlds were separated by language, politics, economics, or decisions made along the way. Of course, my own world was nothing like Alba's world. I didn't even grow up in the United States, much less in an environment where gangs, drugs, and jail were nothing unusual. I wanted to understand the world from which Alba came, but I also felt unable to comprehend how these experiences influenced her college career. What I did understand, however, was her knowledge that college would be very different from home. I also knew that if I wanted to learn more about Alba, I needed to learn more about my own background, and I needed to engage in what Iris Marion Young called a "sense of wonder."

From my readings, my own experiences, and my interactions with Alba, I theorized that she needed to "be on both shores at once" (Anzaldúa, 1987, p. 78) and become adept in juggling multiple identities and oppressions. Her home language (Brandt, 1990; Guerra, 1998) is different from the language used in school, a language that she needs to acquire if she wants to be successful in a competitive society. According to Deborah Brandt (1990), "the school, a middle-class, majority-run institution" (p. 107) disadvantages students who are "deemed to be at risk in school literacy performance to the extent to which their home language is at odds with the so-called explicit, decontextualized language of the school" (p. 106). Juan Guerra (1998) put it well when he pointed out that "members of the group must come to terms with the tension that results from their varied attempts to accommodate their practices to and challenge the constraints of the discourse community in which they operate" (p. 61). I found that Alba had to digest new information and also had to acquire new and unfamiliar literacies—accommodating and challenging—in order to become adept in using academic discourse conventions.

It is easy to say that Alba needed to juggle multiple identities and literacies, and I have often discussed this in my writing. I can easily relate to confusions of boundaries, but it is more difficult to make assumptions about how Alba saw her identities at home and in school. But it is probably safe to assume that Alba could relate to the following question and answer that Lilian Bridwell-Bowles (1995) asked about her "lily-white" history: "So what does it mean to write or to learn to write from multiple perspectives? From a personal perspective, my life has been directly touched by racism, by war, by AIDS, and by the feminist movement. As I have been touched, I have changed and my language and my rhetoric have changed" (p. 55).

Alba tells me that "I guess it's more of a struggle for someone of my class to make it to the university than it is for, say, someone from the middle class." But Alba does not think that the additional burdens will deter her from succeeding. She is convinced that "if you study, and you do, then you can get by, so you can get that degree." Alba wants to succeed in a community that does not fully embrace her. And despite her acknowledgment that she is going to face more difficulties than Anglo middle-class students, she is convinced that she can overcome these difficulties and achieve the "American Dream."

I still consider getting my doctorate an accident. I was never overly confident that I could do it, and could do it successfully. My initial fears about being an imposter are still ever present. I just know how to hide them better now. Alba's self-assured attitude, despite the problems she seems to be facing, is foreign to me. I have often asked myself whether I was right about what I considered "indulging" Alba in her allusion about the "American Dream." What if she can't succeed? But then, why would I even make such an assumption?

Alba started college full of positive attitudes. Nevertheless, she didn't think that she was a good writer because her writing in high school had never received any positive feedback: "I don't think I knew how to write well, I mean I was taking an English course at the university at home . . . for writing skills before I got here, because I was scared. My papers really weren't that well, and I was just really criticized." Her placement into a two-semester course at the university reinforced her perceptions of being a "basic" writer, needing extra help. It broadcasts to her and the university community that regardless of her college admission, she does not fit in.

Many of my instructors used red pens when correcting my papers. The comments were overwhelming, and I considered quitting many times. My ESL classes were helpful, but they did not prepare me for the "real world" of academic writing. I thought I could write adequately, and I wasn't prepared to be "underprepared" and to be told that I had definite language deficiencies. But I could easily attribute this to my "international" status. Alba, on the other hand, was in a different situation. She went through the American school system but did not receive the same training as those supposedly better prepared for college.

Alba's placement into a basic writing course and her designation as "lacking" literacy skills should not come as a surprise. Her background sets her apart; it enables her to see things differently, to move outside the prescribed standards, to be critical of oppressive forces. But it also enables others to view her differently, and it disadvantages her in a university setting. Alba's real-life experiences are discounted in a setting that values decontextualized and abstract literacy and at the same time brands "groups who emphasize the concrete and contextualized" as deficient (Brandt, 1990, p. 109). Additionally, as Suzanne de Castell and Allan Luke (1988) pointed out, the "social, cultural, and political consequences of a national literacy which is based on imposed, rather than derived, culturally significant information" exclude those members of the community whose background is not specifically based on "American language, culture, and economic life" (pp. 173-174).

I cited Brandt, and de Castell and Luke because I thought that their concepts of literacy would help me understand the possible reasons for Alba's placement in a basic writing course. In the end, however, I wanted to follow Min-Zhan Lu's (1992) argument that "individual consciousness is necessarily heterogeneous, contradictory, and in process" (p. 889). But the university had apparently not yet moved away from "theories of acculturation and accommodation" and did not necessarily encourage diverse students' voices in all classrooms (p. 910).

## RHETORICAL STRATEGIES IN CLASS AND ONLINE

At the beginning of the semester, Alba blended in with the rest of the students enrolled in the basic writing course. She usually sat at the far end of the U-shaped room, next to another Latino student with whom she spoke in Spanish. She checked out her peers and the instructor, but she hardly ever participated in class discussions. It was difficult to figure out whether she was paying attention or was thinking of something else. Did she do the readings? What *was* she thinking? These questions did not just apply to Alba; many students did not participate extensively in class activities. The easiest assumption is that they were bored or didn't do the readings and therefore had nothing to contribute to the discussion. In Alba's case, it turned out that she was not at all disinterested in the topics discussed in class but that the classroom environment, especially at the beginning of the semester, did not seem to provide the needed space for her to express her opinions without feeling intimidated and out of place.

I now realize that my questions left out the obvious: If Alba had negative experiences in her one university writing course, and if most students were told that they were "underprepared," why would they want to participate in a classroom setting where the teacher might consider them "outlandish"? And, when considering my own college career, I certainly did not trust my teachers to understand where I was coming from. I always expected the worst, especially when it came to writing. I knew without looking carefully at graded papers that once again I had points deducted for using wrong prepositions and for using subheadings in a literature paper. I would have loved to wear a baseball cap and pull it over my eyes so that I could hide from my teacher.

Alba's behavior was in accord with studies on nontraditional student behavior with which I had become familiar early in my academic career. According to Patricia Bizzell (1987), students who have not been trained in White, middle-class values have more difficulties adapting to academic requirements (p. 297). A similar argument is brought forth by Shaughnessy (1977), who discussed the split between literacies acknowledged at home versus those acknowledged in a school setting (p. 3). David Bartholomae (1987) concurred with Shaughnessy and called for providing students with tools for success in academic life (p. 69). Additionally, feminist researchers have pointed out the increased vulnerability that women associate with being outspoken in a classroom setting. To provide a more congenial learning environment for women, scholars have repeatedly called for less adversarial classroom discourses, considered especially important for women students whose socialization process has conditioned them in ways often associated with less aggressiveness, an unwillingness to speak up, and a tendency to be conciliatory (see, e.g., Kramarae & Treichler, 1990; McCracken, 1992). Alba, however, overcame these barriers, and she was able to speak up. But it was not face to face in the classroom. Instead, she chose to speak out online, where she could take time to formulate and organize her thoughts. Her participation during the various online discussions showed consistency throughout the semester.

Everything I read fit perfectly with my understanding of Alba's position at the university. Her story had all the ingredients that showed her as a victim of an elitist system that does not acknowledge the positive impact of difference and diversity. Alba was poor, she was an involuntary minority, and she was a woman. I was able to use Maureen Hourigan (1994) who, in *Literacy as Social Exchange*, called for specificity and for "studies that consider the intersection of class, gender, and culture" (p. xviii). By working with Alba, I could try to come to some preliminary conclusions about how her background influenced her critical thinking and writing. And because the class used online discussion forums, I could also try to make connections between a student's background and her use of computers. Additionally, my predisposition to argue against the dualistic notions of male and female discourse strategies led me to hope that Alba would show more assertiveness in her interactions in class and online.

## ONLINE COMMUNICATION STRATEGIES: CRITICAL THINKING AND IDENTITY POLITICS

In the basic writing course that Alba attended, students were especially encouraged to reflect on their own experiences and to explore and share their "living literacy" with class participants. Susan Romano (1993), Alison Regan (1993), and later on Suresh Canagarajah (1997) and de Montes, Oran, and Willis (2002) show that online forums could indeed help students be more vocal about class-related issues and could induce them to engage in critical thinking online. I also argued in earlier publications (Gruber, 1995, 1999) that teachers who used online discussions needed to learn how to let go of the impulse to control the classroom because students were less likely to respond to teacher questions and comments in online forums than in a face to face environment.

By drawing on students' knowledges and experiences, this socialization process was intended to provide a fuller and more complex picture of the participants than usually achieved in a classroom where time constraints and curricular activities do not allow for extended explorations of students' backgrounds, their struggles with university requirements, or their activities outside the classroom. Alba, like other participants in the online discussions, used the online forum to inform classmates about her ideas and to let them know her position on issues of immediate concern to her. After reading an article on Latinos in higher education, Alba acknowledged her "otherness," and used it to define her position as a nontraditional student. She showed that she identified herself with other Latino students whose situation on college campuses was mainly characterized by an exclusion from mainstream culture. She wrote the following:

> There are approximately 6% Latinos in the state of Illinois who pursue a higher education each year. The population of Latinos out of 40,000 who attend the University of Illinois is only 4% to 6%. The article that we read reflects the reasoning behind the sad statistics. Strong family ties, homesickness, guilt because you feel as though you are abandoning your family. All this aside from the fact that minorities in general are consistently confined to attending public schools with low funding and overcrowding. Thus Latinos are unprepared to attend the universities of their choice without being a step behind. True, there is the old saying "no one is going to hand you anything, you have to earn what you want in life, and work hard for it." But isn't it a shame that some should have to work harder than others because of a biased injustice—ethnicity. No one can help who they are, what their ethnic background is, the only thing you can do to help better yourself is get an education. This is especially pertinent to those of us who have no other outlet or don't come from wealth. An education is all we have but it is unfair when being who you are or believing in your culture and how you were raised becomes an obstacle. I as a Latina cannot help who I am. God gave me this gift and I thank him for it everyday. I will never try to hide or deny who I am. If I ever did I believe it would be impossible. It is in my name, my speech and my golden brown skin. I love my family and my culture, but I've posed a goal to become a doctor and I know there are many hurdles before me. But I like my forefathers want to achieve something and maybe, in the process, try to make it a little easier for Latinos in the future to go to college. I am a first-generation university attendee, so is my brother before me who will graduate next year. There were none before us, but there will be many in my family to come.

This comment seems to show acute awareness of her status as a minority student who, despite the supposedly equal opportunities at the university, has to work harder and fight against stereotypes associated with Latinas and Latinos. Alba sees education as a means "to make it," to be successful in a White-dominated world by aspiring to the goals upheld by the majority in this society. However, despite these aspirations, she also pointed out that she does not want to sacrifice parts of her identity and deny her background. Instead, she emphasized her position as a Latina student and used this to show her determination to gain access to educational goals usually denied to people from nontraditional backgrounds.

I constructed Alba's extensive comment as her willingness to share her background with the rest of the class, facilitated by the online forum. These online discussions provided me with an opportunity to "listen" carefully and to take another look at Alba's self-evaluation as a writer. It was very clear that Alba had thought about her ethnic and cultural background and was willing to be critical of an unjust system that provides advantages to the mainstream while at the same time making it more difficult for those on the fringes. For Alba, being a Latina seems to incorporate a number of conflicting positions that she addressed in many of her postings. Family values, poor schooling, and negative stereotyping by others are among the issues that she addressed.

It is interesting how her comments in this post and in later posts reflect some of the issues addressed in recent scholarship. For example, Nancy Barron (2003) in her *College Composition and Communication* article pointed out that one of the biggest challenges for Latinos is "learning *to do school* and achieve some learning as individuals while also maintaining a sense of self as defined in their homes and by their groups" (p. 12). The problem, Barron, pointed out, is that "we seem to accept that we know enough about each other, so, really, the only point in coming together is to be heard but not really to listen. Asi son y ya. That how they are, y ya" (p. 16). Alba attempted to write about the problems she and other Latinos faced in school, but it was difficult to know whether somebody was really listening to her comments. Would she experience the same problems of voicelessness—despite her articulate comments—that advocates for a less racist and biased society have experienced? She seemed to know that her ethnicity and her background put her at a disadvantage at school, but she also indicated that she was proud to be who she is. Her comments remind me of another section in Barron's work. As Barron (2003) put it, "we believe, mostly unconsciously, that we've entered school at a deficit because we're involuntary minorities" (p. 20). Alba wants to erase this deficit and become a doctor. Will her perceptions of herself and of the other make it more challenging to achieve this goal? Or will it be solely a question of academic skills? In other words, will her self- and other-perceptions hinder or help her success as a student?

If we look at nationwide statistics, less than 30% of Latinos finish their undergraduate degree in 4 years, and less than 50% finish it in 5 years or more (Swail, Cabrea, and Lee, 2004, p. 26). The dismal statistics colored my questions about Alba's success: Will Alba's determination be enough to get her through school, and to get her through courses where she might feel stereotyped or ignored or picked on because of who she is? Will her family need her? Will she be able to connect school and family without running into conflicting obligations? These questions also influenced my interpretation of Alba's comments in the online forum.

I saw the idea of succeeding by "claiming an education" (Rich, 1977) run throughout Alba's entries. Her concern with the effects of unequal opportunities in education, which she sees based on unequal opportunities on a larger scale, provoke her to post an entry geared toward making others aware that nonmainstream students have to work harder to achieve the same goals as mainstream students:

> I seriously feel if we had the opportunities that everyone else did (like attending private and or schools in the suburbs which have up to date educational curriculums and equipment) we wouldn't be so behind in comparison thus terminating the unfair advantages and supposed segregation because of it according to the so-called scholars.

As a researcher and scholar, I have often addressed the unfair disadvantages that Alba talks about. I read Swail et al.'s (2004) findings that only one of four Latino students were academically prepared for postsecondary education, and that the risk factors faced by Latino students far outweigh those of Anglo students (pp. iv-v). When I consider my own positionalities as a teacher, however, I am not sure whether I can be seen as participating in creating better opportunities for nonmainstream students. I am still working through the question of whether it is enough to create a syllabus that allows for different learning styles; whether it is enough to raise awareness about issues of diversity and discrimination in classrooms or at conferences; whether it is enough to build students' confidence by encouraging them in their writing endeavors; whether I pay attention to the larger picture of discrimination that makes it difficult for minority students to even get to college; and whether I listen and wonder enough, or whether I just want to be heard?

I wanted to listen, and I wanted to wonder about Alba's identities. Online, she identified herself as a disadvantaged minority student, but she also identified herself as a woman who still does not have the same opportunities as men. Similar to her rhetorical strategies in her entries on her ethnic and economic status, she was assertive when discussing the role of women in American society.

> I think it's about time someone is finally addressing the issue of equality of the sexes, particularly in the school system. Males are constantly being granted more funding and support for activities and academics when women have as much right to it as they do.

I was very interested in Alba's comments on gender issues. Many times, young women at the school where I conducted my research were not overly interested in establishing their perspectives on gender in their first year of college. It was more important to figure out dorm life, sororities and fraternities, and newly developing relationships. Alba's comments seemed to show greater insights than I expected. This was, of course, another moment when my preconceived notions of college freshman were undermined by Alba.

The complexities of Alba's identities could also be seen in her interest in the school system and the status of bilingual education in the United States:

> Sink or swim, that is the school system without a bilingual education curriculum. . . . Bilingual education aids in the preservation of the already existing native culture and the formation of the new medium of the new societal standards.

This comment related to Richard Rodriguez's article on bilingualism in the United States, which class participants read for class discussion. This entry leaves little room for doubt about Alba's position on the U.S. educational system and its tendency to value school literacy over home literacy. Her opposition to Rodriguez's idea that acquiring a public identity necessitates losing one's private identity becomes even more distinct during an in-class synchronous discussion on that topic. During this discussion, Alba concluded by stating:

> prefiero murir parada de que vivir de rodillas
> I rather die standing than LIVE ON MY KNEES- Zapata
> I rather die living the way I choose; with freedom, than live out my life by someone else's standards!!!!!!!!

I realized, through this entry, that Alba could write in Spanish—it was the language she spoke at home with her family—and in English—the language associated with the "public" identity Rodriguez discussed in his article. However, instead of denying her private identity, she defined herself as a Latina whose identities are inseparable. I saw Alba as living proof of Houston's (1992) argument that nontraditional women's experiences are the result of their interlocking oppressions and identities that they bring to the academic setting. She showed an ability to draw on her experiences and to include information on aspects of her life that influenced her development as a nontraditional woman student.

Alba's own experiences as a student, and her mother's insistence that she needed to be taken out of bilingual education classes, did not deter her from arguing for the benefits of bilingual education. Alba did not divulge much information about her own schooling, but her comments seem to indicate her strong support of bilingual education. Nationwide, this support is dwindling rapidly. The expiration of the Bilingual Education Act in 2002, and recent propositions supported in various states have supported English-only laws, and have made it more difficult for teachers to address learning difficulties based on language difficulties (see the special 2002 issue of *Rethinking Schools*).

When I read Alba's entry, I was not sure whose standard she was addressing in her commentary. I don't even know if this entry is an indication that she considered college "someone else's standards" or whether she addressed her comment to larger societal ills. According to earlier comments, her own standards for living her life include becoming the first medical doctor in her family. Because of my own perspectives on "standards," and because of my more cautious attitude toward the limitations of living the way we choose, especially if we choose a profession that is full of standards, I saw Alba's comment as being that of somebody whose idealism was laudable but would have to be adjusted to the realities in which we all operate.

Alba also seems to draw on her experiences in a discussion on the use of negative stereotypes in commercials. During this exchange, students voiced a variety of opinions, mainly defending the freedom of advertisers to produce any commercial they wanted. Eric, for example, did not see the negativity of the ads, and even after an extended discussion, he was unwilling to concede that stereotypes are perpetuated by advertisers. Thus, Eric posted an online entry that reinforces his belief in the freedom of advertisers:

> I feel the use of "Frito Bandito" and the tall Mexican guy in commercials was not discriminating. This is because they were not negative figures. The advertisers even commented that they were trying to add humor to the commercial. Maybe the advertisers chose to use the tall Mexican guy because corn chips were originated in Mexico. This would add to the viewers that these are authentic and that makes them better than other corn chips sold by other companies. Personally I think it works because right now I'm going back to my room to crunch on some "Frito's."

Beverly Daniel Tatum (1992) might see Eric and Alba as individuals whose racial subjectivities have not yet been fully formed. As she pointed out in "Talking about Race, Learning about Racism: Application of Racial Identity Development Theory in the Classroom" and also addresses in *"Why Are All the Black Kids Sitting Together in the Cafeteria" and Other Conversations About Race* (Tatum, 1997), we all move through different stages of racial identity development at different times in our lives. Eric seems very comfortable making assumptions about the reasons why the advertisers chose a "Mexican guy" to sell their corn chips. Tatum (1992), in explaining the formation of identity and White privilege, pointed out that white students who become aware of racism experience disintegration and later reintegration into the status quo, re-establishing a belief system that supports the "overt or covert belief in White superiority" (p. 15). Eric's comment could be seen as the comment of somebody who did not see a problem with the ad because it wasn't a problem for his group. He might have wanted to establish his position as different from the position of a racial minority, or he might not have considered the impact of racism on of his classmates.

Alba's opposition to Eric is clearly evident in her detailed response to his comment:

> Eric, I guess it's easy for someone who has never experienced negative stereotypes to not see how one can find the Frito Bandito ad offensive. It is very easy to say it shouldn't bother you when you haven't experienced it. You can't possibly know how it feels for some one to say or imply negative things about you if it never happened to you.
>
> Eric, I never asked to be born who I am, just like you never asked to be born who you are. You see we didn't have a choice. But I'm proud of who I am, and fortunately and sometimes unfortunately we do have the choice of thought and perception and how we express it. It is too bad that in this society someone can use that choice and power to publicly try to demean someone else. Latinos aren't all Bandito's or as it means in English-thieves. How someone could use that as a ploy to try to entertain and then sway humorously to buy a product is not funny. It is the abuse of negative perceptions like that that make it hard for someone like me to believe those who try to say you and I are equals. I know better and know that we are, because my family instilled equality and positively reinforced my self perception. Unfortunately not everyone was raised like myself, and therefore not everyone is going to dispel the advertisement as a fallacy. There will be children who will believe, there have been children who have believed.
>
> I am your equal, therefore I deserve the same respect you do. I am entitled to not be the object of one's failed attempt at comedic advertisement, that really shouldn't be funny to anyone!

Alba's comments indicate experience with racism and racist attitudes. She admonished Eric for taking the ad so lightly without looking more closely at the underlying racist implications. In Tatum's (1997) words, Eric would need to abandon "individual racism" and he would need to recognize and oppose "institutional and cultural racism" (pp. 94-95) to advance to a higher state of racial identity development and to arrive at a more fully integrated racial identity. What I was most impressed with in Alba's entry was her willingness to engage in a conversation that, according to Tatum (1997), is very difficult for students to have because the results of such conversations might not lead to positive interactions but instead might harden already existing positions. Alba could not assume that Eric learned much from this exchange, but if we believe Iris Marion Young's (1997) assertion that dialogue "teaches us about the narrative histories and interests" of each other and that such interaction allows us to "construct an account of the web of social relations that surround us and within which we act" (p. 58), then we can see their exchange as a starting point for learning more and understanding the social realities of each other. Alba, in this exchange, was willing and determined to let Eric, and the rest of the class reading her postings, know why her position on the ad is so markedly different from the one Eric took. It provided her with an opportunity to respond to what she considered an uninformed and racist comment triggered by an advertisement. And she also indicated with this posting that she was willing to fight for equality despite all the hurdles put in her way by school administrators, teachers, peers, advertisers, and politicians.

Alba's repeated emphasis on her background is quite different from a group of Hispanic students discussed in Susan Romano's (1993) article in *Computers and Composition*. Romano pointed out that when exploring *Los Vendidos*, a play about Mexican-American farm workers, none of her students with Hispanic surnames "identify with any of the Mexican-Americans in the text" (p. 12). She argued that "evasion of experience encountered now, here, at this university, constitutes a decided disinclination on the part of the marginalized to occupy that subject position and a disinclination on the part of the dominant to respond to such a move" (p. 19). However, she finds that one of her students, Elena, although not publicly defending her identity, acknowledges her ethnicity: "What I feel is that it's worth losing your 'hispanic Identity' to society, just remember, you'll never lose it within you" (p. 26). Alba, on the other hand, not only remembers her "Hispanic identity," but also is quite confident online to announce her opinions.

It was interesting to read about Romano's experiences in the classroom she described. Most of my experiences were quite similar to those expressed by Romano's students. In many cases, students seemed to be more comfortable expressing their ideas and opinions about the touchy subject of race and ethnicity within their own groups. As Tatum (1992) pointed out, students who have not moved through the various stages of racial identity development often immerse themselves into their own racial group and actively seek to work with members of their own group (p. 11).

Alba, on the other hand, not only emphasized her own struggles as a nontraditional student; she used her knowledge and personal encounters to make her classmates aware of the unjust American social and political systems. Her entry on violence in Chicago—a topic that was of immediate concern to her—shows her identification with, but also removal from, life in the ghetto:

> I am the product of an environment you could call the Ghetto. Or in politically correct terms an underprivileged area. I was on a day-to-day basis surrounded by violence. I grew up with many of those who committed such violent acts as murder and if I were to go home at any time and encounter any of my old "kick the can" partners I would politely carry on a conversation with some of them who haven't died or aren't in jail. Violence to me was just an everyday life occurrence. I think about it sometimes and see the irony of it all, how my life has just grown accustomed to witnessing death and violence. My ears have grown numb to the gun shots, the names of the day's fatalities. Somehow one tends to just tune it out until you witness it personally and you contemplate how maybe it could have been you. On the night of April 15,1994 two friends of mine were nearly fatally shot. I even held one in my arms as he lay shedding blood and passing out from the loss. I didn't hear the screams at the time and still it all feels like just a bad nightmare. I remember trying to hold my boyfriend back from going out and trying to find those who had shot our friends. I remember the blood on my shoes, the ones I threw away. I remember the leather jacket I carried with a bullet hole the size of a compact, the one that would never again be used. I remember almost fainting in church the next day. I remember the phone call to my friend's mom, "I'm sorry your son's been shot." I don't remember being scared for myself but for my boyfriend's safety. These are things I vaguely remember. But, I know I'll always vividly remember the cold sweat nightmares I had of seeing my own violent death—but then again how could I ever forget. I sleep with them every night.
>
> This is the experience of witnessing violence everyday and occasionally first hand. There are no real ways to describe it so one who hasn't lived it could understand. I don't really try to understand myself. I guess those who haven't should just be fortunate and Thank God

> we're alive and pray for the safety of those we Love. Because I know this isn't isolated to where I live, Violence is everywhere it sees no color, wealth, poverty, it has no religion, it just exists and we all should be wary.

It is difficult to describe my reaction to Alba's online entry. I had no personal experience with gang violence or murder, and I was hoping to keep it that way. Of course, Alba did not ask to grow up in a violent environment, and I did not ask to grow up in a small town of 900 people. The question then is how do I discuss Alba's experiences and the possible implications of her experiences on her academic success? Nowhere is it more important to remember Iris Marion Young's (1997) admonition that we cannot achieve symmetrical reciprocity in our relationships and that it isn't even useful or advisable to try to know what the other person goes through. Instead, I always need to remind myself that I need to know how to listen, and how to listen carefully. What, based on the information provided by Alba, was I able to learn about her experiences? I didn't ask her any follow-up questions because I thought that I would be intruding on her privacy and that it might be painful for her to talk more about her experiences. Now I understand that my silence might have been an indication of not being interested in Alba's story or of assuming that I knew what Alba experienced. Neither one was the case from my perspective, but I also did not allow myself to learn more "about the other person's perspective" (Young, 1997, p. 53). Instead, I went away with preconceived notions about the "ghetto" and Alba's experiences with violence.

I don't know what Alba experienced. I heard and read about it—gang violence, poverty, housing projects, joblessness. But I have never lived in the ghetto, and I don't know what it means. I have many questions about it, and I can listen to those who have lived with violence and death. How, though, can I be sensitive to my students' needs without assuming that "I know where they are coming from," or without coming across as uncaring and unconcerned about the larger political, historical, and social implications of such revelations? How do we ask questions, as researchers and teachers, that allow both parties to learn from each other and to listen to each other without the often debilitating effects of preconceived notions?

I approached this entry as a researcher focusing on aspects of language use. For example, Alba's ironic use of "politically correct terms" seemed to show her disillusionment with calling a part of the city "underprivileged" without trying to create an environment that would make the term obsolete. It also seemed to show her awareness of double standards employed by politicians and people in power who talk about those "on the other side of the fence" but who do not want to work on really understanding the problems faced by this underprivileged, and often times powerless, part of society. Alba also used the online forum to make her readers aware of the inequality in American society; her use of sarcasm and repetition established rapport with her audience, and it also made them aware of what her life is like once she leaves campus. Of course, some researchers would disagree with calling Alba's entry a conscious rhetorical strategy based on conscious choices. If we look at Walter Ong's (1982) ideas in *Orality and Literacy*, Alba might be considered closer to the stage of orality and thus less analytic, abstract, and proficient in literate excursions because she used repetition and parallel constructions to get her point across. Ong, of course, used this argument to diminish the linguistic complexity of Black English, a language that he considers not as highly developed as Anglo-American English and that is, by implication, inferior. However, instead of relying on Ong's dichotomous view, which upholds the "great divide" between literacy and orality, I analyzed Alba's use of language in terms of Bleich's (1988) and Brandt's (1990) situation-based interpretation of literacy in which attention is placed on the process of literacy acquisition, making it necessary to look at what Brandt called the intersubjectivity of "interpretation and meaning in literate as well as oral exchanges" (p. 30). In other words, it is important to look at the situation in which discourse takes place and at how a discourse act is realized depending on the setting, the participants, as well as on the medium used. Alba's use of lengthy messages, her tendency to make "statements," her assertive communication style, and her aggressiveness when defending her background have to be seen in connection with her appropriation of online spaces to inform participants about herself, and to also reflect on her own positionalities as a student and as an involuntary minority.

I continue to appreciate Alba's willingness to write about her position on identity, race, ethnicity, gender, and class even more after reading Nancy G. Barron's (2003) article. She asked, "How many academics (Anglo and of color) understand how difficult it is for students of color to talk about color, maybe even about the mainstream, to an Anglo?" (p. 25). I grew up in an environment where people would gladly discuss the political, historical, and social reasons for any problems we faced—at the grocery store, over lunch, in a coffee house, or on the street talking to a neighbor. But I had not experienced the entrenched fears that often disabled individuals from different backgrounds to talk productively about race and racism.

Alba often used the online forum to make other class participants aware of who she was, what her status at the university was, and how her situation was the result of her position as a nontraditional female student.

Writing online seemed to allow Alba—whose gender, ethnicity, and class background have traditionally excluded her from those who are accepted in the college classroom setting—to be critical of discriminatory academic standards and critical of the dominant power structures. She tried to increase her classmates' awareness of a nonaffluent Latina's struggles in a largely hostile academic context. Two students, Jay and Miriam, expressed their appreciation of being able to acquire a better understanding of other cultures and other people's struggles:

> I am glad that I am in this class because I can receive different opinions from all types of people. At my school everybody had the same opinion or just didn't care about going into great detail if they did conflict. (Jay)

> I found out a lot of information that I never knew before. I feel like I am much more informed on the idea of being a minority, and the ideas that go behind it. (Miriam)

What seems to become evident from Alba's interactions and comments is the need for a pedagogy that Eugene E. Garcia (1999) described as a responsive pedagogy that "argues for the respect and integration of the students' values, beliefs, histories, and experiences, and recognizes the active role that students must play in the learning process" (p. 157). Garcia saw the advantages of such a pedagogy as a way to expand students' experiences and to use these experiences to approach new knowledge. He also maintained that teachers need to include in their teaching a familiarity "with the cognitive, social, and cultural dimensions of their students' learning" (p. 158).

Through my research, I tried to show the various dimensions that contributed to Alba's learning. Alba's upbringing, her grandmother's insistence on getting a job, her mother's emphasis on education, her growing up in an economically underprivileged area, her father's machismo, her desire to become a doctor, her position as a Latina student—influenced her discourse strategies and her literate behavior. Similarly, I wanted to show, through self-reflexivity, that my interpretations of Alba's comments are influenced by my ideologies, my histories, politics, cultural background, economics, and international status, and they are situated within specific constraints based on my experiences, my understanding of Alba's history, and the history of race relations in the United States. Using a self-reflexive approach to research, shedding light on how the personal influences the professional, is my attempt to acknowledge that we need to pay close attention to how we are situated by others and how we situate ourselves as researchers, teachers, or administrators.

In the next chapter, I take a close look at Celie's background, her interactions with her peers, and my initial approach to discussing her background and her interactive behavior. I show again the need for reflecting on the choices we make as researchers, and for incorporating information that sheds light on our diverse roles as researchers and teachers.

# 4

# STRIKING STRAIGHT

## LEARNING TO DO SCHOOL AND BE COOL

And when we speak we are afraid
our words will not be heard
nor welcomed
but when we are silent
we are still afraid
So it is better to speak
remembering
we were never meant to survive
—Audre Lorde (1978, "Litany for Survival")

I first read Audre Lorde's "Litany for Survival" in 1989. At that time, I was struck by the despair and despondency expressed in the poem. I saw it as an expression of hopelessness that I had never experienced to such an extent. I knew about being ignored by teachers and peers. I also knew that I got upset with myself when I didn't speak up during conversations and discussions. But I never connected my actions and inactions to an existentialist position on survival. Lorde's poem took on additional meaning when I read Lightfoot's (1980) comment that "young black girls are an ignored and invisible population," and that "they are a human resource that does not even deserve social and cultural imagery" (p.139). Survival, gaining voice, and becoming visible were fundamental underlying concerns when I worked on this chapter. I was hopeful that 25 years would have changed the bleak picture expressed in Lorde's and Lightfoot's comments. I was also hoping that June Jordan's (1985) call for acknowledging the diverse populations in the United States had been heard. As she pointed out, "this invisibility and this silence of the real and various peoples of our country is a political situation of language that every one of us must move against, because our lives depend on it" (p. 6).

When I decided to look closely at Celie, an African-American woman, I was hoping to contribute a small slice to making visible the invisible. Of course, I know that Celie's experiences cannot be seen as representative of the experiences of African-American women on the campus where I conducted my research or on other college campuses. But what she seems to have in common with many African-American female students, despite decades of civil rights efforts, is her "invisibility" in a mainly Anglo environment. She also shares a long and turbulent history of precarious race relations in the United States. The Civil Rights Movement achieved many inroads into changing American politics; however, people's attitudes are difficult to change, and racist attitudes are unfortunately long-lived. John Ogbu (1988) supported this view and argued that because of preconceived notions about African Americans, "black education . . . has usually been inferior, often separate, and generally based on white perceptions and stereotypes of black status in society and especially in the economy" (p. 236). African Americans have not been able to achieve equal status in the United States because, as he argued, they are considered "castelike" or "subordinate" minorities who "are either incorporated into a society more or less involuntarily and permanently" and are "generally regarded as inherently inferior by the dominant group, who thus rationalize their relegation to inferior social, political, economic, and other roles" (p. 231). Unfortunately, books such as *The Bell Curve* (Herrnstein & Murray, 1994) remind us of the unjust and arduous struggle that African Americans are still fighting in order to achieve equal status and equal education in American society.

When I entered the United States educational system for the first time in 1986, I was only peripherally aware of the current inequalities in the American educational system. I had read about the history of slavery, reconstruction, *Plessy vs. Ferguson*, *Brown vs. Board of Education*, and the Civil Rights Movement. But similar to my understanding of the results of World War II on current political and social movements in Austria, my understanding of how unresolved historical events created inequalities and influenced race relations was an academic and theoretical one. I learned, mostly through reading, that prejudice and stereotype often define cross-cultural and cross-racial interactions. When I looked into research on the situation of Black women, I found the comments by the Combahee River Collective (1982) especially interesting and useful for trying to understand

Celie's position at the university. As they pointed out in "A Black Feminist Statement," "Black women's extremely negative relationship to the American political system (a system of white male rule) has always been determined by our membership in two oppressed racial and sexual castes" (p. 14). Similarly, Michele Wallace (1993) called the outcome of Black women's oppression the "structural 'silence' of women of colour within the sphere of global knowledge production" (p. 119). The silencing of Black women and their "negative relationship" is not only confined to the political realm but carries over into the educational system as well. I appreciated Constance M. Carroll's (1982) comments when she pointed out that

> there is no more isolated subgroup in academe than Black women. They have neither race nor sex in common with white males who dominate the decision-making stratum of academe. Black males in academe at least share with white males their predominance over women. (p. 118)

bell hooks (1981) helped me connect Celie's individual comments during our discussions with the macro-structure that influenced her childhood and her education. hooks specifically discusses the hierarchical construction of human interaction that, according to her, puts black women at the bottom of the social strata, oppressed not only by White men and women, but also by Black men (pp. 52-53). hooks (1984) continued this argument in her later work and pointed out that Black women comprise "the group that has not been socialized to assume the role of exploiter/oppressor in that [they] are allowed no institutionalized 'other' that [they] can exploit or oppress" (p. 14). Of course, hooks' argument could be refined further to acknowledge oppression by class structure, economic status, disability, or sexual preferences; however, her work contributed to raising awareness of Black women's general oppressed status in a race-conscious and prejudiced country.

Celie, an African-American woman who grew up in the inner city and who was a first-generation college attendee, was categorized as underprepared and "at risk" by the academic institution she attended. Like her classmate Alba, she was placed into a basic writing class to provide her with extra training in how to write academic papers. Like Alba, her "lack" of academic literacy marked her as somehow less qualified, less intelligent, less equipped for success, and like Alba, she was classified as a "remedial student," carrying all the negative connotations associated with the term. However, Alba and Celie were also very different: They brought different cultural knowledges to the classroom, different assumptions about the university environment, and different ways of dealing with their "outlandishness." Celie brought to the classroom a wide variety of literacies; however, according to her test scores, they were not the privileged literacies and were therefore not part of her placement into an academic writing class.

I included Celie in this discussion to give her a voice in the struggle for recognition. Her presence in this chapter will hopefully contribute to what Michele Wallace (1993) called "the 'production' of knowledge, the structure, content and 'circulation' of the 'text,' as well as the 'audience' of consumption" (p. 119). At the same time, I want to acknowledge how my own positionalities produce knowledge that has been filtered by my understanding of race relations, historical and political events, as well as the position of involuntary minority women's positions in academia. In other words, by providing readers with a close analysis of Celie's words and actions, and by highlighting the reasons for my own approach to this study, I hope to contribute a small part to increasing my own as well as my readers' understanding of Celie's position in an educational setting. Celie's story, like Alba's story, is the story of an individual, but it is also the story of someone who has grown up with historical, political, cultural, and social assumptions that in many cases determine educational and economic opportunities.

I wanted to place Celie within the larger historical reality of exclusion and racism to raise awareness of her complex status at the university and the multiple barriers that she has to overcome to become successful in an academic environment. I was interested in her perceptions of her position at the university, and I wanted to find out how she defined herself in terms of her gender, her African-American heritage, and her social and economic standing. Like Alba, her complex identities and her outsider status at a mainly White university seemed to relegate her to the periphery of the academic discourse community. My own interpretations of Celie's complex identities are based on her comments about her family, her comments on her academic position, and her online comments on race and gender issues.

I realized during my research and when I started to analyze Celie's comments that her background and her interactions could easily and simply define her as a woman, as an African American, or as a basic writer. But I also realized that the interconnectedness and interdependence of these defining characteristics necessitated a research approach that would take into account the complexities of Celie's situation at the university. I am hoping that this chapter contributes a piece to a jigsaw puzzle, where the finished product consists of many interlocked individual pieces that—upon careful examination—reveal a larger, less fragmented and more complete piece. Similar to Selfe and Hawisher (2004), I want to make sure that I don't suggest that Celie's culture is "simple, discrete, or monodimensional" (p. 129) but that instead it is "complex, overlapping, and shaded by many factors such as gender, socioeconomic status, and geography" (p. 129).

## EQUAL BUT SEPARATE

As a composition teacher, I mostly look at students' writing based on their performances in the classroom. As a researcher, I want to analyze students' performance in the writing classroom by taking a close look at their writing and trying to make connections between their writing skills and their social, cultural, and ethnic backgrounds to understand how their writing is influenced by their home and school literacies (Brandt, 1990). I now realize that it is quite easy to take for granted the need for analyzing students' literate behaviors from a macro- as well as a micro-perspective. However, it is not so easy to admit that as a researcher, I have jumped to conclusions about a research participant's background based on my own limited interactions with the participant, and on my understanding of history, social relations, politics, gender, and race. When I worked with Celie, I knew that how I viewed the world might not be the same as Celie views the world. To clarify some of my assumptions, I try to contextualize Celie's work in a composition classroom, and I also try to contextualize my work as a researcher by looking carefully at my underlying—whether rational or irrational—assumptions about my research and about Celie's participation in my research.

Celie was from a south suburb of a big midwestern city, where she grew up with her mother, a certified nurse's assistant at a hospital, and her father, who did "miscellaneous jobs" as an electrician and a plumber. She had two brothers and three sisters, but she was the only child of both her parents. Asked about the others, she wasn't quite sure what the situation was. She explained how they were all related:

> my oldest brother and sister is my father's. O.K. It's me, my oldest sister, my oldest brother, and my baby sister, they are all my father's kids, and the other brother, that's my brother from my mother.

When I asked her whether her father got married a second time, she laughed and just stated that "no, but that's a different story, no, we are not gonna go into that."

Celie was also uncertain about her brothers' and sisters' careers. She only knew that her brother Clyde was in the service and was about to become a father. With the others, she said,

> I don't know what they're doing. My sister, I have a sister who's also 18 years old, she, she's in the Navy, she went to the Navy, and my sister Gina, my oldest sister, she has three girls, but I have no idea where she's living or what she's doing, she is kind of struggling, and my oldest brother, he just got out of jail not too long ago, I don't know what he did to get in there, but we don't even associate with him too much, and my baby sister, I don't really know too much about her either, I just know she exists.

As a researcher, I wanted to make sure that my subjectivities about Celie's background only entered peripherally into my interpretation of her family history. But it would be naïve to think that I didn't impose my own family history onto Celie's history. I don't think that Celie could relate to my stories about my family background. When I told her that I had a sister and four brothers, and that we were very close, Celie didn't seem too curious or too impressed. I wanted to find some commonalities between Celie's and my own background, but having six kids in the family didn't cut it. Although I live on a different continent, I knew exactly what my siblings were up to, and I knew that neither one of them ever considered the army as a potential job opportunity after having to serve their mandatory military training at age 18. None of them had done anything that would put them behind prison bars, and at that time neither one had any kids. My parents got married in the 1950s, and they are now getting close to their 50th wedding anniversary. For Celie, family was defined differently because of her experiences, her interactions with her parents, and her connections with her brothers and sisters. Celie knew that one of her sisters was struggling, and she also knew that there was no money in the house. However, she described herself as lower middle class, because, as she puts it, "we got a lot of nice stuff, so you could say like middle, but lower middle, cause we broke, we don't have any money."

I tried to understand Celie's hedging when she talked about her class background. I never had any problems letting people know that I came from a blue-collar family. Most of the time it would have been more appropriate to classify myself as a black-collar kid because my dad's work as a blacksmith and later on as a machinist always meant that his blue overalls were covered in black grease. My mother was never able to get his clothes completely clean, although she boiled them on the stove before she put them in the washing machine. We had lots of "things" too that we used for playing outside or inside—hay bails where we played hide and seek, old newspapers that we used to make ocean liners, sticks that we used as swords, wooden blocks that became houses, and a sewing machine that my mother used to make clothes for all of us. We might not have been the most fashionable kids in the neighborhood, but we were always clean and fed. I do remember my mother mentioning one time that my father's parents weren't overly enthusiastic when my parents married because my mother's family was considered poorer than my father's family. They could only afford to keep a goat, and my father's family could afford a cow. My parents made sure to always have a cow and a few pigs, but we never had a goat in our backyard.

I wondered whether Celie's emphasis on being lower middle class despite being "broke" showed her unwillingness to see herself as less privileged than her peers, reinforcing Elspeth Stuckey's (1991) assertion that "the idea of a class structure is uncomfortable for many Americans" (p. 1). Instead, Americans "live the mythology of a classless society" which "provides equal opportunities for all and promises success to those who work hard to achieve it" (p. vii). To illustrate this point, Stuckey used Michael Harrington's description of steelworkers:

> If you ask the unemployed steelworkers in the Mon Valley about their social class, they do not have a moment's hesitation. "We pay the taxes and take care of the kids and go out for beer and pizza," a steelworker's wife—an activist in her own right—insisted. "We're middle-class." (cited in Stuckey, 1991, p. 3)

Celie's concept of being middle class, then, seemed to be less an expression of her parents' economic status than an expression of a more general dislike to be seen as less than middle class. It might be that Celie or Celie's family connected class status with success and upward mobility. It might be that college signified middle class to her and her family. It might also be that middle class meant "things," or that Celie never thought very seriously about economic or social class as a signifier in her life. Maybe in her neighborhood, they were considered quite well to do. In my own neighborhood, we were pretty much the same as everybody else except for the five families that owned big farms. My mom used to work for one of these farmers when she grew up, and she didn't have a lot of good memories about that time. My own experiences certainly had an impact on how I interpreted Celie's comments about being "broke" and middle class. And maybe I didn't know enough about Celie and her family to know what it meant for them to be broke but still have things.

From what Celie told me, going to college was never an option but an expectation. The only point of discussion was the kind of college she would choose—a big 10 school or a historically Black university. Her high school of about 2,500 students was "not very diverse at all," she pointed out. When I heard Celie say that, I automatically assumed that most students and teachers were Anglo and that she was one of the few who did not fit the majority profile. I assumed that she knew what it meant to be an outsider, and I assumed that she would have experienced racist comments, stereotypes, and unfair treatment throughout her high school career. My assumptions were based on my, albeit limited, experiences in the American educational system. I knew that the student population of the one university with which I was familiar was largely Anglo, and I knew that most of the kids in the K–12 system in the small town where the university was located were also Anglo. But when Celie continued that "about 90% of the students were African American," I realized that I could not assume that Celie was always a racial minority and that Anglos were always the majority. Celie, in other words, was a member of a majority group in her school. She wasn't "different," she wasn't "outlandish," she wasn't an "alien" in her community. She liked her school, she did well, she was "normal," and she didn't have to think about fitting in because she was in already. In some ways, Celie's experiences during her high school years were similar to my assumptions when I came to the United States. Celie did not consider race as a stumbling block when she started to think about college because she didn't have experiences that would have led her to believe that she might run into race-related problems.

When I came to the United States, I had my own concepts of what it meant to be American. If people grew up in this country, if they had a passport, a driver's license, or a birth certificate, they were Americans. I was not an American, and my international friends who were in the United States on visas or work permits were not Americans. I had not yet accepted the different nuances of being an "American." Only recently, a Latina colleague mentioned that only internationals considered her "an American," and that other Americans designated her as a Latina, Hispanic, or Mexican American. Although she grew up in the United States, she never saw herself as American because she was always seen as the "other" in her own country. Celie was not the "other" when she went through her K–12 education. She grew up in the United States, but she only experienced a small part of U.S. culture and politics. Race was not her primary concern when she went to college. In some ways, she seemed to be as unclear about how race and color influence people's perceptions as I was when I tried to grasp the complex layers of race relations.

It seems, however, that Celie's mother was aware of the problems that Celie might face at a mainly Anglo campus. But Celie told me that she and her father thought that an Anglo campus would be more useful for Celie's education:

> This is the story, ok, when I was, I'd say 7th or 8th grade, I wanted to go, I said I was going to go here [university], and me and my father, we went to the Northside one time, and I told this old little white man that I wanted to go here when I go to college, and he said, well, that's a very competitive school, I don't know if you'll be able to get in there, you got to have the grades and blah blah blah blah, and I was like, I'm gonna get the grades, I'm gonna get there, you know, I want to go here, and so when I got older, when I went to high school, [...] my mom said to go to a black university, cause she felt that maybe I would feel more comfortable at that institution, and I will probably get more out of it, but then, I don't know, it was a whole bunch of other options coming my way, but I still ended up coming here, because, well, my father had a lot to do with it, because at first he said you should go to a black university, then he said, well, I guess, when you get a job, it will look better if you graduated from like a big 10 university than from a black institution, not trying to put it down or anything, but it just look better, on a, you know, applications, so, I thought about it, and I decided to come here after all, this was my first choice, and it was also my last choice to be.

When I read Lisa Delpit's (1988) argument that almost any African American who has become "successful" has done so by acquiring a discourse other than the one into which he or she was born (p. 292), namely the dominant culture's discourse, I could see Celie's and her father's motivation for going to a Big 10 school. In a larger context, Celie's and her father's value systems—that White schools offer better chances for future employment—might be influenced by the historical inequalities in educational opportunities addressed, for example, by W.E.B. duBois (1903/1982), Anna Julia Cooper (1892), and later on Constance Carroll (1982), bell hooks (1981, 1994), Cornel West (1993), and Jacqueline Jones Royster (2000). For example, Constance Carroll explained that Black women "choose education and the hard struggle of career mobility as the 'way out'" (p. 119). This also means, said Carroll, that these women follow "tacit formulae" to succeed in academia:

> You must be *better qualified* than the men.
> You must be *more articulate.*
> You must be *more aggressive.*
> You must have *more stamina* to face inevitable setbacks.
> You must have *more patience*, since you will advance *more slowly.*
> Above all, you must remain *feminine* and *not appear threatening.* (p. 124)

Being a woman in educational and other settings still carries a high number of disadvantages. Being a woman and being Black, the "double jeopardy" addressed by Carroll, puts Celie at a disadvantage before she even came to college. Although a transition from high school to university might not be a dramatic shift for some students, Celie's experiences as a member of the majority in a mainly Black school during high school, and her realization that she has now become a minority seem to make her transition even more challenging. The sudden switch from majority to minority, as hooks, Carroll, and others pointed out, can result in a loss of self-confidence as well as alienation. According to Carroll (1982), Black women in majority Anglo environments "have few role models with whom to identify in developing healthy self-concepts" (p. 119). Similarly, hooks (1989) maintained that "often black women are such an 'invisible' presence' on campuses that many students may not be aware that any black women teach at the university they attend" (p. 60).

Celie was not hampered by the many studies that pointed out that she would most likely be at high risk as a college student. Celie, instead, was intent on succeeding. This was especially important to her because she was the first one in her immediate family to go to a university. When I talked to Celie at the end of her first year, she pointed out that her impressions of the university after a year on campus were mainly positive and that she had adjusted to campus life. She considered it "a real nice school" with a diverse student population where one could meet Asians, Asian Americans, Latinos, Indians, and people from all over the world. However, this surface-level fondness exhibited at the beginning of our conversation changed when she talked about specific classes. Despite her proclamations about the diversity on campus, she was less positive and upbeat about the integration of the different backgrounds. She did not accuse her peers of racism, but thought that

> they probably are just ignorant, I wouldn't say a racist, but I got to say they were accustomed to different cultures from what I came from, they just knew about themselves, and the people that they were, they

> grew up with, they grew up in a smaller town, they didn't know about other cultures and all of that, like, I said I had security guards in my school, they say, wow, what did you do, you know.

Although Celie started out by telling me that she liked the school, she became increasingly critical about the university's and students' inability to work together and to cross ethnic and racial lines. She remembered an incident where she felt uncomfortable because the people to whom she was introduced did not welcome her into their community:

> I mean I feel comfortable going to this school, but like hanging out with different groups of people, I don't feel comfortable, cause I have a friend who is Indian, and she says, Celie why don't you go to this party with me, Celie why don't you come here, it's like, and so I went with her one day, and she was with her little, her other little Indian friend, they would introduce me to these other people and I felt like, very uncomfortable, because they probably, I mean I felt like they were looking at me, like who is this black person, why you came with her?

Celie was not the only one who found her peers "ignorant" and distant. Anne DiPardo (1993), in her discussion of an adjunct program at what she called "Dover Park" University, found similar attitudes in the student population of the observed school. The excerpts from one of her focal student's description of his experiences as a first-year student at his university show the similarities between his experiences and the experiences of Celie. Al, the student interviewed by DiPardo, pointed out:

> The first day that I came in, I felt as if people were looking at me, and staring at me . . . they asked me where I was from. And when I told them, then, you know, they looked at me crazy, you know. I guess they just knew I was from Southwood and I was supposed to have been in a gang or something. (p. 134)

Al's alienation took its toll on him, and although he finally found acceptance in a Black fraternity on campus, he no longer expressed any desire to get to know people from other ethnic and cultural groups (p. 136).

Al's disillusionment seemed to be mirrored in Celie's experiences, and although nobody suspected her of being in a gang, she had to deal with similar feelings of alienation that were expressed throughout the interview. In one of her smaller classes, Celie was especially aware of her "different" status.

> I was the only black person, not only the black person, I was the only black *female* in the class. It was a Chinese person, and a Latino. We sat together, and then there was, everybody else, and everybody else was white and they lived on farms, and, I mean, seriously, they lived on farms and . . . this is their first time interacting with black people on a whole, and that was real stressful for me, considering that the first topic that we talked about in there was racial diversity, and it was like, my TA [Teaching Assistant] didn't know how to approach it either, cause she wasn't going to say, like certain things that might offend me and then, the rest of the students, or some of the students in the class, they were kind of ignorant with the, you know, when you try to tell them something, they play around with it, it was pissing me off.

I interpreted Celie's situation as fitting the description of hooks' (1994) "native informant" who, because she is the only African-American woman in the class, is objectified and considered the representative of all the things associated with being African American (p. 43). I also saw Celie's experiences as similar to those of an African-American student discussed in Helen Fox's (2001) book, *When Race Breaks Out*. As this student put it, "Towards the middle of the semester I began to feel resentful at the role I was selected to play. I did not enthusiastically embrace the occasion to help broaden the views of my white peers." (p. 97).

I certainly do not know what it means to be seen as the sole spokesperson for African Americans in the United States. The histories, prejudices, and stigmas attached to this descriptor are very different from those attached to my nationality. But, as the only Austrian in most of my college classes, and as the only Austrian faculty member in my college, I have often been considered the representative of everything Austrian. In other words, I am the authority on Austrian politics, social life, history, and culture and customs. It does not matter that I am from a small, isolated place where everybody talked politics, but where politics did not evolve around national or international events but small-town business such as moving the middle school to the next town because there weren't enough children to keep the one in our town open. I could talk about social life, which meant visiting with the neighbors or relatives up the street or getting dressed up for a barn dance. I did not know that big towns and cities had libraries and museums until I went to high school. I was definitely an expert on history, but it was a history told by my grandfather and my parents. I knew all the stories about how my grandfather escaped from a Russian internment camp during World War I, and I knew that during World War II my father and the neighbor—who were both 17—hid in the woods so that they would not have to go to war. I heard about the priest who was taken in and interrogated because one of the parishioners told the Nazis that his sermon was anti-Hitler. And I know that the same parishioner was the first one to donate a lot of money to the church after the Nazis were defeated. I could certainly discuss our customs, but it might not be the customs of the rest of Austria. I doubt that my family is representative of the rest of the nation, and, like Celie, I can only represent myself and the small slice of knowledge—always eclectic and subjective—that I picked up along the way.

My supposed expertise was almost always a positive asset with my peers. They did not have negative connotations that would make my life more challenging. But Celie struggled with her position in an unsupportive environment, and she almost convinced herself to drop the class that made her feel uncomfortable. Unlike my position as a "native informant," Celie had to deal with the often negative connotations of being Black *and* a woman. Celie seemed to slowly learn—implicitly or explicitly—that she was part of a long history of negative race relations, and that her gender and race were a "double jeopardy" in the classroom, which, according to Beale (1970), refers to an African-American woman's simultaneous racial and sexual oppressions. However, despite her discomfort in the class, Celie decided to remain in this section for lack of other opportunities. But, she related that she felt on the spot constantly, being scrutinized for all her words and actions, feeling that she would have to do better than the rest of her classmates to prove their assumptions about her wrong.

Celie was not only annoyed and stressed by being under constant observation and examination; it also influenced her interactions with other class members. She started to feel increasingly alienated:

> in the class, it was like, the minorities sat on one side, and the whites sat on the other, I mean it was divided, and it remained divided, I guess they probably knew each other, it was like, they knew each other and we knew each other, but we never really like got a chance to find out about one another, you know, I mean, we didn't like, ask questions, I guess, . . . some of the more impossible ones, I don't even want to deal with them, cause they were ignorant.

Her position as the only African-American woman made her situation in the class precarious because she felt that her opinions were discounted most of the time. She became disinterested and tried to disengage herself from the class discussions because she did not want to be upset all the time:

> it was boring, because, it wasn't like, I mean it wasn't like it was enough input from everybody, it was majority white in the class, so you got a white perspective on everything, sure enough I'd say what I had to say, and they showed me my respect to my face, but every once in a while . . . I hear them say something negative, you know, but they would never say it so that I could hear it, but I mean it was like, . . . it became one voice instead of the voice of different backgrounds, so when we talked about different topics it was like, basically, you know, how can anybody be so ignorant?

These feelings of institutional separation were not only part of Celie's experiences. bell hooks (1989), for example, remembered her years at different universities, all characterized by hidden racism and sexism. She related that many of her professors and peers "communicated their message in subtle ways—forgetting to call [her] name when reading the roll, avoiding looking at [her], pretending they do not hear . . . and at times ignoring [her] altogether" (p. 57). What they expected, she maintained, was that students from marginal groups "learn obedience to authority" (hooks, 1994, p. 4). Furthermore, hooks argued that "those . . . from marginal groups who were allowed to enter prestigious, predominantly white colleges were made to feel that [they] were there not to learn but to prove that [they] were the equal of whites" (p. 5). Celie's experiences seem to be similar ones, and she is stressed out because she feels that she has to prove herself constantly in her class.

For Celie, it was not only the lack of community among students in a classroom setting but also a feeling of alienation outside the classroom that created tensions in her life. Instead of being comfortable interacting with peers from different cultural and ethnic backgrounds, she noted that students rarely interacted with members outside their own ethnic groups. A friend of Celie's who visited the campus, expressed the problem quite succinctly:

> When I first came down here, I see this as a very segregated school. . . . It is by people choosing it to be, because like this group of blacks hanging together and this group of whites, and maybe these groups of Jewish and the Arabic, you know, everybody is just separate . . . and they don't speak.

In the course of our conversation, Celie's enthusiasm about the school became more subdued, especially when she discussed specific classes and specific incidents in which she felt unwelcome and out of place. Her doubts about school reminded me of Henry Louis Gates' (1990) discussion of minority students in "The Transforming of the American Mind." These students, he wrote, "say that they feel like visitors, like guests, like foreign or colonized citizens in relation to a traditional canon that fails to represent their cultural identities" (p. 35). In other words, although Celie considered this a great university that offered a lot of opportunities, she also acknowledged that the realization of these opportunities might be more difficult for students outside the mainstream. In her words, most people were "ignorant" toward other cultures and did not seem to be interested enough to learn more.

## BASIC WRITING AND ONLINE COMMUNICATION

Celie took my basic writing course during her first semester at the university. Unlike her other classes, this course had a diverse student body, and many of the discussions were conducted online. Celie mentioned that she felt comfortable in the class and that she liked to participate in the online discussions. She described it this way:

> I liked [the class] . . . because it was like a combination, a mixture of everybody, it was like, maybe a few people here of one color, and a few people, I mean it was like, it was, equal, it was even.

Celie was usually a few minutes late. She looked tired and overwhelmed, and it took her a while to start concentrating on the tasks at hand. Some days she seemed dazed by all the expectations imposed on her—writing summaries and short responses, participating in class discussions, getting to know the instructor and the students, and learning a new technology. She acknowledged this in an online posting 3 weeks after the beginning of class:

> My experience, so far in this class, seems to have had a rocky start. I am not necessarily sure how things will end up for me. But I am hoping and I am praying that things will go better for me. It seems as though now that I am doing a little better considering the difficulties that I have experienced. . . . I hope soon things will begin to pick up for me and I will try to resume my duties [with] more responsibility.

She emphasized her struggles when she pointed out that "I think I am starting to take my baby steps. But every once in a while I tend to [fall] right back down."

Celie did not mention why she experienced problems with adapting to the new environment. I thought that it needed little explanation. Her position as a newcomer to an "alien" territory; her status as a minority woman; her placement into a basic writing course; her sociology, chemistry, and math courses, all took their toll on her—her energy and productivity seemed to wane. It did not seem that Celie's prior experiences prepared her for the experiences on a college campus, most likely because she was going through the process of acquiring specific and yet unknown academic discourses. Her experiences did not seem to fit with the experiences necessary for school literacy. School, as Deborah Brandt (1990) pointed out, is a "middle-class, majority-run institution which is symbol-intensive by nature" (p. 107). Celie's difficulties might then be attributed to her struggles with a literacy that did not come naturally but needed to be acquired by taking "baby steps."

I am no longer so sure that Celie's difficulties were the difficulties of somebody who was unprepared for academic discourse conventions. Thinking back to her comments, Celie and her family knew that she would go to college. She never mentioned that her high school did not prepare her for academic success, and she was sure that she would succeed in academia. She might have had school literacy, but she might not have been able to successfully address the home literacies that were not part of her academic literacies. Celie seemed to realize that she was considered different by the majority, and that she did not fit the campus population's concept of insider. I remember my own disenchantment after being in an American college classroom for the first year. I considered myself adequately prepared to participate fully as a student, but my accent and my ESL errors in my writing soon classified me as other than mainstream and in need of additional help. My prior university experiences, and my acquired academic knowledge, no longer mattered. In addition, my contextualized home literacies were no longer part of my academic learning experiences. They had become a liability and burden more than a positive and useful asset.

The writing course that Celie took, unlike most college courses that I took, attempted to address topics that might be of interest to a highly diverse student body. Once Celie realized that she could use her contextualized and concrete knowledge to contribute to class discussions, she became more involved. Many of the articles that students read included topics that addressed the positions of minority students on college campuses, racism, and women's struggles. Celie, as a basic writing student in a mainstream educational, cultural, and social system, seemed to find those topics interesting and useful. I saw June Jordan's (1985) comments on the importance of including Black students' experiences as providing an explanation for Celie's willingness to participate in these discussions. As Jordan pointed out, Black students' "language, their style, their sense of humor, their ideas of smart, their music, their need for a valid history and a valid literature—history and literature that included their faces and their voices—all of this was pretty well ridiculed and rejected, or denied to them" (p. 29). I saw Celie as highly literate; she knew how to communicate, and she didn't hesitate to express her opinions when the class discussed topics to which she seemed to relate. This became clear when she got into heated discussions with two African-American men, Bailey and Langston, who she got to know in class and who seemed to make it their responsibility to argue with her and also support her efforts in trying to put her thoughts in writing. Langston read all her papers, and Celie trusted his comments because they addressed similar issues pointed out to her by the instructor. But unlike the instructor, Langston was more direct with his criticisms and told Celie point-blank on one of her papers that she needed to shape up and work on her writing skills. And although Celie was really hurt and chided Langston for his insensitivity to her efforts, she saw it as her goal to prove to him—not the instructor—that she could do better. The interaction styles of the three students were very similar. None of them minded being teased, and none was afraid to let the others know exactly how a specific comment made her or him feel. I am not sure if Celie could have had these interactions with students who were not African American. In other words, it is difficult to project whether they were comfortable with each other because of their race, because they grew up in similar neighborhoods and could relate to each other, because they all felt like outsiders at the university, because they were in the same class, or because they had a similar sense of humor. In any case, Celie was comfortable talking with Bailey and Langston, but she was often reluctant to chat with other students in face-to-face interactions.

Celie became very adapt in using the online discussion forum for interactions with the instructor and her peers. One of the important features of electronic communication for Celie seemed to be the informality of the responses, employing what Hawisher and Moran (1993) called a "language that is somewhere on the continuum between spoken and written language" (p. 630). For Celie, posting online did not imply formal written papers; instead, she could explore aspects of her literacy that would not be acceptable in formal papers and that would also not be used in spoken language. In a sense, Celie could be ambivalent about using academic discourse, and she could incorporate into her responses the "multicultural context" of her life (Lu, 1994, p. 448). Her online voice became a voice among many other voices. I saw her voices, in connection with the voices of other participants, contribute to what Brandt (1990) called "creating a pluralism of voices." This pluralism, as Brandt pointed out, "not only requires that many voices be heard but that the differences in those voices be understood" (p. 124). She further argued that the variety of voices can become "the catalyst for sharpening everyone's literacy" (p. 124). The online environment seemed to enable Celie to explore her voices and at the same time to listen to other participants' voices. She seemed to become involved in a community of learners who all had different opinions, who didn't mind arguing, and who were ready to defend their positions. Min Zhan-Lu (1994) would argue that Celie and the other students in this course were able "to hear discursive voices which conflict with and struggle against the voices of academic authority" (p. 448).

## A REBEL IN MORE WAYS THAN ONE: CELIE'S ONLINE COMMUNICATION

For Celie, the online forum became a medium that she used to discuss her identity as a student who did not always fit in. This was especially apparent in her response to an article on Latino students on college campuses:

> As I read through the selected reading, I realize that Latino Americans has as many problems with discrimination as with any other minority race in this country. They especially have a lot of similar problems as do African Americans. On a college campus, that is of a predominantly white race, the Latino Americans have to understand that a lot of times their institution is nothing like how it was at home. They have run into a whole new ball game. It's hard enough to understand the types of new things that are taking place on campus that they are not use to. But when there is an addition of people who are always trying to bring you down whether or not it is subtle or very obvious it doesn't make thing any easier. The action that Latino Americans took was that they formed an Affirmative Action group in order to make sure that things are made known to those people who are unaware of the everyday problems that their people have to face. This group was also formed to address to their people the importance of maintaining their heritage and to be true to themselves. But their struggle to achieve is

just as strong as everyone else. And they want to be treated just as fairly as the next person.

Celie did not read the article as an abstract and theoretical piece on another group's difficulties. Instead, she drew connections between her own experiences as an African-American woman and the experiences of Latino students. When I read her entry, I saw a student for whom the college campus was an alien place, especially because members of the "predominantly White race" discriminate against Hispanics, African Americans, and other "minority races." Celie's entry reminded me of bell hooks (1994), who in her work could have had Celie in mind when she discussed the constant identity struggles that face minority groups. As hooks said in *Teaching to Transgress*:

> Those of us from marginal groups who were allowed to enter prestigious, predominantly white colleges were made to feel that we were there not to learn but to prove that we were the equal of whites. We were there to prove this by showing how well we could become clones of our peers. (p. 5)

Min Zhan-Lu (1994) addressed very similar concerns about students who are forced to acquire a specific kind of academic discourse, one that ignores the multiliteracies that students bring to the classroom. Celie's entry seemed to address this bias toward an accepted norm. She showed a strong antipathy against "those who are always trying to bring you down" and a strong identification with minority students who have to struggle in an outlandish community.

My own experiences with outlandish communities were manifold when I moved to the United States. Everybody and everything seemed weird to me. I met American students who invited me to coffee, but they never would follow up on their invitation. I was asked to go to a professor's office, but it was not to be told that my paper was really poorly written. He wanted to chat about the topic I wanted to write about for my final project. My American roommates shouted at the TV during football games, and they did all-nighters before exam time. All that wasn't normal behavior to me, but it didn't influence me negatively and it didn't bring me down in my academic endeavors. My problems in school seemed to originate from my fear to speak up and my use of wrong prepositions and tense when I wrote my papers. I didn't have American friends who would help me out, and I often thought I was the only one who struggled to make it through her courses. Everybody else was much smarter and much more articulate. So I found myself isolated from the majority community, and I found my support group with other international students. We realized that our experiences in this foreign environment were quite similar. We could talk for hours about how different it was to have to explain your background because nobody knew where you were from, and because they made assumptions about your country that were far removed from your experiences. None of us knew how to interact with Americans; actually, we all believed that Americans were not interested in us in the first place. I don't know if they wanted to bring us down, but I know that I did not feel welcome by them. I don't know how Celie felt. I know what she told me, and I know that she had problems in her classes and at the university in general. She told me that she attributed her difficulties largely to her race and her gender. And scholars such as hooks (1994), Carroll (1982), Royster (2000), and others have pointed to similar distressing experiences.

Not all online discussions in which Celie participated centered around education or were part of the original syllabus. For example, the class decided to discuss gang violence after a student, Olivia, brought an article to class that discussed a drive-by shooting in Denver which was targeted at a gang member but unfortunately killed the gang member's brother. Responding to the reading, Celie wrote:

> I wasn't shocked by the article but I am upset by it. I don't understand the purpose of why a gang feels they can solve their problems by shooting someone. And then if they mess up and shoot the wrong person, what have they accomplished then?

I was, and still am, shocked by gang violence, shootings, lootings, murder, and rape. I get upset when I hear about police brutality, the Korean store owner who killed a kid because she took a soda, one gang going after another one. And, what I should emphasize too, I only hear and heard about this. I have never been in a situation where I got pulled over and repeatedly beaten by a police officer; nobody has pulled a gun on me and threatened me because I wore the wrong color shirt, and the stories about gang initiations are just that—stories. In general, I agreed with Celie when she argued that the problem did not only lie with the gang members but with society as a whole:

> People are aware that there is a problem. It's just that some are too afraid to stand up and try to make a difference. Or maybe they just don't know where to start.

Celie was not alone with feeling frustrated. Langston, for example, thought that an incident like the drive-by shooting in Denver would not even be reported in Chicago because, as he said, "drive-bys are too common. It's like printing that the moon came out and was in the sky." He expanded on this point:

> We should hear about it but there are only so many pages in the newspaper and . . . the news only lasts, at most, an hour. It's not boring to hear about it, it's just sad to ALWAYS hear about it. We can't do anything about it, only the killers can. We've tried to influence them enough and we shouldn't stop but, there comes a point where the killer and only the killer will have to lay the gun or knife down. We can't do it for them. (Langston)

Gang violence was a topic that concerned both Celie and Langston, and both expressed their frustrations with the attitudes of those who were not directly confronted with it, and they also admitted the powerlessness that they experienced in these situations. After the in-class discussion, Celie continued her postings and pointed out that the problem was exacerbated because of widespread ignorance. With this, she expanded on the impact that violence has on society:

> I feel that young people today don't realize how serious of a problem gang violence is. Maybe one day our young people will wake up and see how some of their reasons for "regulating the problem," killing people, are extremely petty. But one never knows, maybe this is part of our fate, "man is his own worst enemy". . .

Although she knew that the reasons for these murders are "extremely petty," she also implied that human nature seems to thrive on self-destruction and violence.

What was interesting, but mostly to be expected, was that Celie and Langston approached the topic very differently from the way I approached it. Neither Celie nor Langston mentioned the larger historical, political, and social forces that make space for and often fuel gang violence. How, for example, do poverty and unemployment impact the actions of young people? Does police brutality reinforce violence? And how does language about gang members influence our perceptions of who they are? When do we glorify gangs, and when do we condemn them? When do we blame the gang members, parents, community, and state laws for violence? I wanted to find answers to these questions, most likely because I didn't know how else to approach the topic. Celie and Langston are more interested in how gang violence influences their own lives and the lives of those close to them.

Unlike Alba, Celie did not indicate whether she had experienced gang violence. When I read Celie's entries, I made the assumption that because she grew up in an economically depressed neighborhood in a big city she would have experienced gang violence. In a sense, I made similar assumptions about her background that people made about my background. Once I knew that she was from the inner city, I assumed that she would have come in contact with gangs and violence. But this assumption was completely unfounded because Celie never mentioned gangs in our talks, and she never addressed violence on a personal level. My version of American inner-city life originated from television and readings, and I also projected Alba's experiences onto Celie. I had not lived in a big city in the United States and only knew what I had been told. I am now amazed at how easy it was for me to take a stereotype for granted without questioning the underlying assumptions about what it means to live in certain neighborhoods, what it means to be Black, or what it means to grow up as a woman. I have argued many times against essentializing the experiences of students based on their gender, race, class, or sexual preference, but I was not immune to it myself when I forced my perceptions of inner-city life on Celie's experiences.

It helped me understand the problems with my own assumptions better when Celie responded to *Do the Right Thing*, a Spike Lee (1989) movie that she had not seen before. She was especially interested in the group mentality that in her opinion led to prejudice:

> I would just like to respond to the racial issues in Thursday's movie. Surprising enough I have never seen the movie. I found it very disturbing that different people view other ethnic groups as being negative towards each other. Everybody looked out for their own people, there was one person who was there to try to regulate every- thing, that was the mayor. At first I thought the movie was going to be kind of stupid, yet after it was over it got me to thinking about all the trouble that could be prevented if there wasn't any prejudice in the world. It really bothers me that people would prejudge another person just because of their ethnicity. It shouldn't matter what their cultural background is and no one but no one should make prejudgments on people before getting to know them. You never know what that person has to offer them.

Celie could have been talking about my own ignorance about her background. I could see myself easily falling into the trap of prejudging Celie because I "knew" that she was from the inner city, and I knew that she was Black. But I did not know what it means to be from the inner city, and I did not know what it means to be Black. As Iris Marion Young (1997) would say, I needed to ask more questions, and I needed to find out more about Celie's background and her experiences without letting my imagination get away from me.

## DON'T MESS WITH ME!

Celie had figured out, after being on campus a few weeks, that being Black in most parts of the United States meant being a minority, and that her high school experience was an exception to the rule. She also knew that being Black and a woman was often even more difficult to deal with. Her comments made it clear that she strongly believed that women did not have the same social, political, and economic power that her male counterparts had. Celie, in order to criticize sexist stereotypes, engaged in online exchanges with several other participants. bell hooks (1989) might have seen her voice, and thus her presence, as a step toward fighting the silence that is "a marker of exploitation, oppression, dehumanization" (p. 129).

When I asked Celie about the session on gender issues, she answered with a big smile on her face: "I thought it was fun, cause I got to cuss people out." She expanded on this statement when she continued her explanation:

> you know how, when we were talking about men and women issues, how it got kind of heated on the computer, and I was like, you don't know what you are talking about, blah blah, blah, remember, this one episode when Alex was talking about something about women don't need to be playing like sports and stuff, something stupid he said, and you know, everybody went out for him, I mean it was fun cause you got to different opinions, people's opinions and stuff, so I guess that was pretty straight.

At the time of this online discussion, students were already familiar with each other and were comfortable talking to each other in class and online. Celie thought it was "pretty straight," and the development of the discussion seems to indicate that students did not hide their opinions and could express their ideas without much restraint. Celie seemed to feel comfortable with her classmates, the classroom atmosphere, and the new medium that she used in order to express her ideas.

Like Alba, Celie was not afraid to voice her opinions online. However, their discourse strategies differed in various ways. For one, Celie was less concerned with formulating lengthy arguments and instead responded quickly and questioned the ideas of other participants by posting short comments and inquiries. During the discussion on gender issues, she was one of the first ones to reply to the initial question by the discussion leader, "Do you think that the role of the woman has changed since [the article "I Want a Wife"] was printed in 1971?" Celie's comment showed that she was "liberated" and considered housewifely duties as a burden.

> Yes Roles have changed considerably since then. This is the [19]90s. People have their own minds made up of doing things. Women nowadays don't play that. We have to be set free of all of those duties of being a submissive housewife.

Celie's firm stance can be seen as an expression of her own position as a female college student. In Celie's case especially, she hardly ever experienced Black women role models on campus. She reaffirmed her stand by responding to Masad's comment who thought that "women are more independent these days than before." Celie responded, "I agree with Masad things have changed [since] the article was written." Celie agreed with other participants but was also not too shy to ask about clarification when she was uncertain about the meaning of an entry or when she was dissatisfied with a comment. She immediately responded to Bailey's posting that "I believe that 'I Want a Wife' glorifies the duties women have done for their husbands and children over the years" (Bailey) and asked him "Bailey, honey explain glorify."

Her familiar tone suggests that Celie knew Bailey well and also knew that he would understand her use of "honey" in this context without being offended or making the wrong conclusions, especially because Bailey's opinions hardly ever coincided with Celie's. Celie furthermore seemed to assume that her classmates would know that she was being sarcastic with this address, an assumption that she could make because of previous classroom interactions and a congenial classroom atmosphere.

Celie aborted the use of this familiar address when she did not get an answer from Bailey. She asked again, this time even more pressing: "Bailey what do you mean by GLORIFY!!!" Her exclamation marks and her use of capital letters were evidence that she was starting to be impatient and wanted to have a response to her question. The nonlinear nature of synchronous online discussions seemed to frustrate Celie who wanted to engage in a one-on-one conversation with one of the other participants. But although different topics were discussed at the same time, Celie and Bailey were still able to continue their discussion. Thus, Bailey answered by defining the word and said, "Celie, glorify means to put in the spotlight or to upgrade."

Celie, however, did not seem to be really concerned about a dictionary definition of the word; instead, she wanted to know more about Bailey's attitude toward women's roles. She was not too thrilled with Bailey's interpretation of her question, and her answer showed that she was by no means ignorant of the meaning of "glorify"; instead, she was perturbed by Bailey's assumptions:

> Bailey, honey, I don't understand how you feel that it is glorifying anything. Because I see glorifying as a positive thing. And all of the duties that were described in her article were moreso depressing to me than anything "GLORIFIED."

This sarcastic use of "honey" and her affirmative and aggressive tone were not unusual for Celie. In many postings, she asserted her opinions without hedging and without trying to be conciliatory or in any way cooperative. She communicated her opinion, but she did not invite Bailey to respond. Celie's directness reminded me of my own interactive behavior, and it also reminded me of being reprimanded for not being polite and circumspect enough when I interacted with students or colleagues. My directness was interpreted as rudeness; however, I had no intention of being rude but only used my acquired discourse style to get a point across. Celie seemed to do the same thing. I saw her as trying to get her point across without following some of the conventions that I seemed to forget constantly. If Celie had said, "Bailey, you might want to reconsider your use of glorifying since mostly this term is used to refer to something positive. My understanding of the reading seems to be different from yours," she would probably be seen as conforming more closely to mainstream discourse conventions.

Celie moved on to get involved in another discussion that had been going on at the same time that Celie tried to "set Bailey straight." The topic discussed involved the decreased need of women to protest their situation because equality had already been achieved. Masad and Egan, for example, pointed out that women had less to protest about now that they had become established in American society—a commonly held belief that was also used for minorities and made its way into government offices and reduced active hiring practices that provide women and minorities opportunities for equal opportunities. Celie, however, did not agree with Masad and Egan. She responded to Egan similarly to her response to Bailey:

> Egan, please there is a lot of things women can protest about. See, by you not being a woman you really wouldn't know.

Celie's accusation and her ad hominem attack did not go unnoticed, and although Egan did not defend himself, Langston called her on that comment:

> Celie, how can you say that Egan doesn't have any input toward women's views? (Langston)

Celie clarified her position and although she moved away from discounting Egan's opinion because he was a man, she was still convinced that he wasn't tuned in enough to discuss women's issues.

> Well, I am not saying that he doesn't have any input on women's views all that I am saying is that he must be ignorant to the fact if he feels that there are less and less issues that women have to protest about.

Celie was not only critical of other participants' opinions and challenged them on their assumptions—like she was challenged on hers; she also picked up on comments that found her approval. Thus, she started a dialogue with John:

> There are more and more men who are starting to do the things that traditionally women have done. (John)
>
> John, are you that type of man? (Celie)
>
> Celie, I would do that if my wife did an equal amount. (John)
>
> That's cool, a lot of couples should be like that it would be less of a problem. (Celie)

During this exchange, Celie and John established common ground, and through relatively short postings, Celie learned that not all her classmates react the same way to questions on gender. These online peer interactions seemed to provide Celie with an opportunity to discuss her own opinions and also to learn from the opinions of others. And nobody seemed to mind that Celie was not adept at being, or did not want to be, polite about her opinions.

In the discussion on gender issues, I interpreted Celie's discourse strategies as very affirmative about her position on women's issues; she insisted on getting an answer to questions that she asked; and she was aggressively defending her position. I also noted that Celie connected her comments to previous postings, and despite the nonlinearity of the discussion, her attentive reading and her quick responses provided room for continuous topic threads. She seemed to engage in selective reading and only picked out the comments that pertained to the specific conversation in which she wanted to be engaged. I saw Celie as adept at working in a new medium and using technology to express her opinions about topics that were important to her. She seemed to understand technology in terms of Laura Gurak's (2004) eloquent remarks: "it is a technology of reading, writing, and speaking, and it brings with it changes in all things affected by human communication, changes in everything from grammar and style to conceptions of community, expectations about speed, differing senses of gender and identity, and new ways to do politics" (p. 193).

## I WON'T PUT UP WITH THIS

Students in this class were asked to discuss the portrayal of women and minorities in advertising. Opinions ranged from granting advertisers freedom of expression to endorsing censorship on offensive ads. Calvin Klein was seen as a shrewd businessman by some and as a child pornographer by others. Commercials for Aunt Jemima syrup were condemned as racist or lauded as presenting a positive image of a Black woman. After readings that pointed out that stereotypes are exploited to get consumers to buy a product, and that little attention is paid to how stereotypes of specific groups affect the members of these communities, students became more conscious about the possible problems of advertisements where women are often portrayed as beautiful and sexy, African Americans as mammies, and Hispanics as banditos. According to Clint Wilson II and Félix Gutiérrez (1985/1994),

> Given the social and legal restrictions on the participation of racial minorities in the society of the United States during much of this country's history, it is not hard to see how the desire to cater to the perceived views of the mass audience desired by advertisers has resulted in entertainment and news content that largely ignores minorities, treats them stereotypically when they were recognized, and largely avoids grappling with such issues as segregation, discriminatory immigration laws, land rights, and other controversies that affected certain minority groups more than they do the White majority. (p. 795)

During an online exchange discussing these stereotypes, Celie saw herself as a potential victim of the stereotypical portrayal of women and of minorities. In one of her entries, she commented on the negative impact created by the depiction of women as lifeless objects:

> I feel that for a woman to be on commercials the stereotype lies within the society as a whole. They try to form an image of what a woman "should" look like and act like but that is of course not necessarily true. It doesn't matter about the money the real issue lies with the women that are not in the commercials. These are the women that people see everyday.

She emphasized several times that although there are supposedly ethical standards in advertising, "the media tries to see what it is that they can get away with." She tried to explain her ideas on the influence of commercials:

> Sometimes with the messages that the commercials make, there is a certain standard that is set for that individual in the commercials. This in turn is passed on the viewer who can take the message any way that they may want. But the down side to this is that if a woman is viewed as a sex-model, how would this make the average female feel?

Celie apparently struggled with conflicting ideas about the powers of advertising. Although she gave viewers the freedom to decide on the value of the commercials, she also was aware that certain representations are unrealistic and harmful for women.

Celie was not only talking about the problems of negative stereotypes in advertising; she was also willing to take action against advertisers and the media who perpetuate these stereotypes. Thus, she pointed out,

> I commend all of these people who are against certain products and what they represent. But what about what the media is trying to pro mote when they use other ethnic background in a negative manner to promote their products? Why not boycott those as well?

Looking at Celie's comments in terms of Freire's (1973) "conscientization," her awareness of problematic social conditions led her to call for further action that goes beyond the classroom and that would make her a critical participant looking for social and political change. She started to realize, to use Freire's words, that society is "something unfinished, not . . . something inexorably given; it has become a challenge rather than a hopeless limitation" (p. 13).

Celie's awareness of the objectification of women and minorities also prompted her to question the attitudes of another participant who saw no problems in buying products from organizations that officially discriminate against minorities. Alex, an African-American student, took the position of an unquestioning consumer, a position the advertising industry is hoping for. As Wilson II and Gutiérrez (1985/1994) argued, advertising "enters the ghetto and barrio with a smiling face to convince all within its reach that they should purchase the products advertised and purchase them often" (p. 802). Alex, an African-American student, following advertising's lead, considers it important to buy products that he likes:

> There might be all kinds of companies that are racist but they know how to satisfy your needs. . . . I know that the KKK [Ku Klux Klan] has done a lot of racial things but I can't change that. I'm bigger then that where I'm not going to stop buying what pleases me. (Alex)

Alex seemed to take a resigned position that allowed him to overlook the implications of racism in advertising as long as his needs were met. According to Freire (1973), Alex's attitudes would be representative of oppressed people who, instead of fighting against injustice, submit to it, and "*adapt* and *adjust* to their circumstances instead of seeking to integrate themselves with reality" (p. 23). Celie, who took a more active position and a position that allowed her to see the potential drawbacks of not protesting institutions and companies that build on the passivity of its consumers, responded to Alex's comment and admonished him for his position and his lack of "race consciousness."

> Alex why would you want to support a product when a manufacturer is against us and everything about us?

Alex, however, was not convinced because, as he pointed out,

> I bet all of you that are saying that you wouldn't buy this or that because of race hatred don't know about all the products you buy. (Alex)

Celie could not induce Alex to concede to her opinion that racism and sexism in advertising have a negative influence on women and minorities. However, Celie's growing concern about the impact of some ads showed that she formed her own opinions and was critical about the perceptions that the media perpetuates. In other words, although Celie was unable to convince Alex, her own understanding of the situation seemed to increase and prompted her to be more socially aware and conscious of the dealings of big corporations.

Celie's strong concerns with the negative impact of stereotypes and issues of racism were not only expressed online; she also used the ideas that were generated during the online discussions to write her final paper on "Racism and Essentialism: The Effects It Has on the People in the African-American Community." In this paper, she addressed the stereotypes and prejudices under which African Americans have to suffer. The media, she argued, have a great influence. Television shows, for example, "show society what they want them to see." She explained this by pointing out that "there has been racism in television shows from the *Amos and Andy* sitcoms to the *One Life to Live* soap operas." Furthermore, she wrote in her paper, "the media also tries to tell society that the African American male is lazy, violent, hostile, lacks motivation, willpower, and brings about his own problems." The views established in some television shows and other views held by society create big problems:

> The African-American point of view is that it is hard enough being born into this country which doesn't socially accept them because of their skin color (Anderson, 167), but it is even harder trying to establish themselves so that they can have a good standing job and they can be a part of the middle class (Anderson, 154, Siegelman, 94). It's harder for an African-American male to become part of the middle class since there is a tendency to require more work for an African American to do because there is already a stereotype of laziness directed toward him (Siegelman, 94). So he must often prove himself to those people who feel that it isn't worth wasting their time investing in the futures of these young African-American people.

In addition to the published sources, Celie interviewed one of her peers, Bailey, who had expressed his ideas on race prejudice during various class interactions and online exchanges. She quoted him as saying, "In order for African Americans to achieve our maximum potential these prejudices that lead to racism must be eliminated," thus using a resource that, like Celie herself, could speak from personal experience and from a long history of race prejudice in the American political and social arena. Using Bailey's knowledge was a realization that learning and literacy acquisition were active and heterogeneous processes that did not only take place in the classroom but happened constantly.

I saw Celie, in her online exchanges, in her interactions with her peers, and in her research paper as being able to establish an identity as a woman who, despite prejudices and "ignorance," worked toward achieving her goal, a degree from a Big 10 school. Along the way, she was able to use her literacies and her knowledge to educate her peers and raise awareness of her position as a minority in a largely White university setting. I related her determination and her will to succeed to Frederick Douglass' (1845) resolve to read and write and to escape from slavery. My analysis of Celie's situation at the university and in the basic writing course, and situating her experiences within a broader historical, political, and educational framework, was intended to make visible what is often invisible. I wanted her voice to signify her presence in an environment that, according to such scholars as Gates (1990), Carroll (1982), and hooks (1989, 1994), has negated her existence and the existence of other African Americans. I wanted to help her "write herself into being," and my descriptions and analyses of her interactions were intended to give voice to Celie as an individual and as a member of a historically discriminated group. I provided glimpses into my own historical, cultural, and political positionalities to put into context my approach to Celie's interactive strategies, her comments, and her opinions.

In the next chapter, I shift the focus from individual students to a group of students to show how I interpreted an online exchange where participants seemed to use their authority to exert power and control over their classmates. I also point out the difficult position of interpreting these interactions as a teacher and researcher who supports dialogical authority, wants to see students engaged and empowered, but is also aware of existing power structures that often undermine a teacher's and researcher's best intentions in changing the system to include diverse approaches to learning and literacy acquisition.

# 5

# REDEFINING AUTHORITY

## TECHNOLOGICAL (DIS)INTEGRATION

When I first read the entries that are excerpted in this chapter, I was not sure how to address the many concerns that I had with the comments students had made during an online discussion of the images and the language used for rape victims. I was confident, based on previous experiences with this group, that the interactions would result in a critical analysis of how rape victims are portrayed, how the media influences the depiction of rape victims, or what the implications of accusing somebody of rape are. But students did not seem interested in critically analyzing the issues that were raised. Reflecting on the entries, I now realize that rape, a very real threat to women on a college campus where statistics place one out of six women at risk for being assaulted by an acquaintance, was not a topic that should have been discussed from a distance. When I read the excerpts, I was worried that the contentious discussion had offended and emotionally harmed some of the students in the class. I saw the comments as largely reactionary, based on attitudes acquired from years of socialization in a culture that provides little incentive to look at issues of victimization and the abuse of women.

The posts discussed in this chapter reminded me of several rape cases that received media attention—such as the case of law professor Anita Hill's sexual harassment charges against Clarence Thomas, the Kennedy rape trial, and the Clinton-Lewinsky trial. Cases such as these continue to undermine women's trust in being able to prosecute their assailant without being accused themselves and without being blamed for their actions. bell hooks (1992) shed light on the reasons for "blaming the victim" when she pointed toward the silencing that takes place in "a patriarchal society that socializes us to repress and contain" (p. 80). Rape, in other words, is an issue that rarely finds expression in public settings, including college classrooms, without leading to conflict and tensions. To discuss rape, and in particular date rape, in a beginning composition class is an undertaking that is not only very difficult to mediate, but is sometimes not seen as an appropriate topic for this setting. Instructors not trained in conflict resolution often shy away from controversial issues, especially when they can cause hard feelings and potential self-revelations. On the other hand, however, it would be naïve to think that controversial issues do not enter into students' academic performance and their professional and personal progress. For example, the fear of being attacked can restrict women's ability to use the library after dark, go to computer labs, concentrate on lectures, and feel safe to walk alone from a campus building to an apartment.

I decided to address rape and date rape in this class because I was convinced that raising awareness and increasing social consciousness on this issue might bring about change and lead to an active reconfiguration of cultural, political, and social structures. But I show in this chapter that such reconfiguration cannot happen without reconfiguring how we understand our roles in a very hierarchical and often authoritarian system where dialogue and critical reflection are often replaced by monologic and highly restrictive authority.

## BUILDING ON THE OLD, WORKING WITH THE NEW: AUTHORITY REVISITED

> The future of our earth may depend upon the ability of all women to identify and develop new definitions of power and new patterns of relating across difference. The old definitions have not served us, nor the earth that supports us. The old patterns, no matter how cleverly rearranged to imitate progress, still condemn us to cosmetically altered repetitions of the same old exchanges, the same old guilt, hatred, recrimination, lamentation, and suspicion.
>
> —Lorde (1990)

Audre Lorde's (1990) words reminded me of a recent discussion with colleagues where we "rearranged old patterns" of control. A senior colleague wanted to push a proposal for an area change through the channels that we had not agreed on. Two younger faculty members, both women, politely told him that we appreciated his efforts but hoped that we could discuss this before the final decision was made. The two of us certainly did not redefine power, but implicitly provided our senior colleague with an opportunity to let the chair know that we were all behind him, that we were happy he had taken the matter into his own hands, and that we would soon present his proposal to the department. When we realized that we had once again not been explicit enough for this situation, and that our colleague had no intention of discussing changes to the proposal, we were disappointed by our failed attempt at productive communication and at establishing our own authority in this situation more succinctly. To make a theoretical distinction, we knew that our colleague had asserted his power by using what Peter Mortensen and Gesa Kirsch (1993) called "authority of office," He was my senior, he "knew" how to get the proposal through the channels, and he "knew" what the upper administration wanted. We, on the other hand, wanted to make sure that our proposal followed current developments in the field. We wanted to use our knowledge of the field—or our "authority of expertise"—to negotiate the content of the program and to present a proposal that would be acceptable to the majority. We had different objectives and goals, but we all tried to use our institutionalized authorities to our advantages.

The distinctions on authority that I am making here are less evident in practice than in theory, as Mortensen and Kirsch (1993) pointed out, because both definitions channel power and uphold current hierarchical relationships (p. 559). Thus, power granted to individuals because of knowledge, and power granted to them because of the position they occupy in society—positions that are dependent on class, race, gender, and social and political status—lead to an authority that has as its goal the domination over others. Academic institutions, as Mortensen and Kirsch rightly pointed out, see authority as a legitimate force that is used to persuade, coerce, and initiate or mandate action (p. 560). My colleagues and I felt "authorized by convention" (p. 560), and we were all convinced that our way to interpret our authority was the right one. The same holds true for teacher and student relationships, Mortensen and Kirsch argued. If teachers use institutionally sanctioned authority, the very role of *teacher* can work to control what students will learn in specific courses, how they learn it, and what grades they receive for their performance. As Todd Taylor (1998) argued, "as long as we continue to operate in a culture wherein authority is still very much a function of class, race, and gender, the most we can reasonably expect to gain is a better understanding of the utter persistence of ideological control as microphysical rather than central" (p. 118). In other words, authority is persistently present in our interactions with students, administrators, colleagues, and other constituencies. My own colleague, a senior member of the department, exercised his control over me and other junior faculty members. His abilities to control the situation by pronouncing his opinion as the opinion of the majority, and our insistence that his opinion was the opinion of the minority, almost led to failed negotiations with all members of the group.

But, I have to admit that I rarely stop to reflect extensively on my institutional authorities, and even though I am committed to engage in dialogue with my colleagues, to establish a participatory classroom, and to promote an actively involved student body, I do not actively look for radical changes to my institutional powerlessness. I often do not reflect critically on my authority as the teacher or the administrator of a large university-wide writing program. Certainly, students and graduate assistants give input that influences the day-to-day activities in the classroom and in the program. But the input hardly affects the larger structure of the course and the program. Students are graded on a strict percentage scale. The course outcomes need to be the same across all sections of the writing program. All instructors need to implement technology in the classroom. Although, like other scholars (e.g., Berlin, 1988; Foucault, 1979; Freire, 1968; Giroux, 1992; hooks, 1994; Kirsch & Ritchie, 1995; Lu, 1992; Selfe & Selfe, 1994), I started to move against traditional definitions of authority and institutional powers many years ago, and although I try to show that institutional hierarchies are not inalienable rights, and that authority can be used to help the powerless, it is often difficult to come to terms with my positions as a colleague, an administrator, and a teacher whose authorities shift constantly. Should I extend the definition of authority to include a group's efforts to build a network against existing oppressions when some group members' goal is to continue these oppressions? Should I interpret authority as a means to change a homogeneous, patriarchal, and hierarchical social and political structure when I am the one who is responsible for keeping a structure in place? Is it useful to reflect on how I use authority with my colleagues and with my students if such reflection is not reciprocated? How destructive can it be to abuse the power and authority I hold?

I ask these questions because I know that my own interpretations of authority, my experiences with different authorities, and my ideological predispositions toward feminist and postmodern interpretations of the world largely determine my positions as a scholar, teacher, and administrator. When I looked at Gerald Graff's (1994) interpretation of authority, I realized that on a theoretical level I am worlds apart from his interpretation but that in reality I sometimes resort to Graff's position on student–teacher interactions. For Graff, there is no question that authority provides a teacher with powers that students do not possess:

> However much we attempt to turn education into an egalitarian dialogue, the superior intellectual authority of the teacher is a given that cannot be sloughed off. That is, there is an *unavoidable inequality* built into the teacher-student relationship, if only because once teachers and students are regarded as intellectual equals there is no longer any reason for the teachers to teach the students. . . . The distinction between teachers and students requires an assumption of hierarchy, an assumption that the teacher possesses some knowledge, competence, or skill that the student lacks. (p. 184)

Graff here sees authority as an exercise in power, a view that makes dialogue difficult to achieve. Instead of seeing education as an *exchange* of information, knowledge acquisition moves from the teacher to the student. Because of his concept of authority as the prerogative of the teacher, Graff is also suspicious of Freirean/critical pedagogy and claims that

> no matter how democratic, dialogical, and open your classroom is, no matter how much you problematize your own authority and decenter the dominant ideological structures, your students will still remain intellectually dependent on *you*, if only because there is no one else present to depend on, and most students will not yet be in a position to be intellectually independent without help—they would not be students if they were. (p. 185)

Graff's concept of authority presents some discouraging truths about how academic institutions see student progress and how some instructors understand their position in the classroom. I certainly do not want to be a teacher who sees students as dependent on her. However, although Graff's comments on intellectual inferiority are especially discouraging to teachers who work to establish students' voices as legitimate expressions of intellectual thought, I do tell my students how to write a successful paper, I give them quizzes, I tell them what academic conventions to use, and I grade them on their work. Similar to Helen Fox (2004), I am uncertain about my position in the academy. Discussing graduate students' academic work, Fox argued that what they "need to learn is the language and values of the academy, its styles and structures, its vocabularies and uses of voice, its relationships with authorities, its attitudes toward evidence, its beliefs about what is worthy of being discussed and what is not" (p. 58). But, on the other hand, she is also aware that current pedagogical practices encourage students to explore their own voices, become critical thinkers, and engage in alternative discourses. This "dilemma," as Fox called it, needs to lead to more rigid questioning about why we do what we do, and why we ask the questions we ask. I want to believe that I can juggle these responsibilities, and that Graff's (1994) use of authority as power over students, or Foucault's (1995) analysis of power and authority as a panoptic pattern—is not representative of my interactions with students and other teachers.

I have attempted to follow a definition of authority that is not dependent on an unbalanced power relationship but instead is characterized by what Mortensen and Kirsch (1993) called an "ethic of care." As they argued, it is necessary to discuss *concepts* of authority to account for the various uses of the term. Accordingly, they promote a *dialogic* model of authority that "presents one possibility for rethinking notions of objectified, stable, autonomous authority," and that is "informed by an 'ethic of care'" (p. 557). Through this coupling of authority and care, Mortensen and Kirsch rejected autonomous authority in favor of a "messy pluralism" (p. 567). This redefinition, in their words, provides a possibility to "resurrect authority and make it more democratic, better suited to voices of both consensus and conflict" (p. 569). Consequently, authority is not necessarily dependent on an opposition of dominant versus nondominant, but can also be seen as an interaction based on the mutual intent to acquire knowledge.

Authority in this vein is not seen in terms of exercising power and control but in terms of enhancing social relationships (p. 566). This dialogic nature of authority and the necessity to be teacher and taught at the same time appeals to my feminist and postmodern sensibilities. It allows me to admit the undeniable presence of authority while arguing that authority could be used without trying to exert absolute power or control. Paulo Freire (1968, 1973), as a consequence, has become a favorite long-term subject in my discussions on egalitarian classrooms and on teaching students to be in control of their lives. I very much believed—and still believe despite all my doubts about whether I can put such theories (or pedagogies) into practice—that

> only authoritarian educators deny the solidarity between the act of educating and the act of being educated by those becoming educated; only authoritarians separate the act of teaching from that of learning in such a way that he who believes himself to know actually teaches, and he who is believed to know nothing learns. (Freire & Macedo, 1987, p. 41)

In some ways, it is not difficult to follow Freire and Macedo's model of authority because I know that I don't know everything. As Freire put it, "it is necessary for the one who knows to understand that no one knows everything and that no one is ignorant of everything" (p. 41). I am happy to interpret this to mean that authority is not the privilege of the teachers but instead has to be negotiated and reassessed by both teachers and students, leading to dialogue, conflict solution, and consensus building.

Most days, I see my role as a teacher and researcher to create and propose spaces where Freire's concepts "might serve to interrogate, destabilize, and disorganize dominant strategies of power and power/knowledge relations and in doing so envision a means of enlisting pedagogy into the construction of a contestatory space where a radical and plural democracy might begin to take root" (McLaren & Tadeu da Silva, 1993, p. 49). Of course, I know that such plurality in any classroom is only possible if I redefine authority in terms of the complexity emphasized in the work of critical literacy advocates and advocates of a dialogic reconceptualization of teachers' roles. Instead of seeing teachers as "superior," I try to see meaning-making as an exchange of ideas that establishes different authorities for different areas of expertise.

In an interview with David Trend, Henry Giroux (1992) also discussed issues of authority in terms of its impact on those who teach and those who are taught. I want to believe him when he said that:

> you can exercise authority in ways that do not establish the conditions for knowledge to be produced and engaged. I would call that authoritarianism. Or you can exercise authority to establish conditions in which a central tension lies at the heart of how we teach. The latter method encourages self-reflection, learning from others, and refiguring forms of cultural practice. (p. 157)

I found Giroux's definition of authoritarian modes of expression and authority convincing and closely related to Mortensen and Kirsch's (1993) distinction between autonomous and dialogic authority. I also found their argument for plurality and the move against autonomous authority appealing because I want to believe—as a hopeful but often lapsing practitioner of critical/emancipatory pedagogy and as a feminist—that power relationships are shifting, and that we can contribute to a less hierarchical and disparate society. I find that the absence of stable and unified entities emphasized by postmodernists lends itself to a reconceptualization of stable subject positions, and, consequently, to a rethinking of dominance and subordination. In other words, I am hopeful that the replacement of a dominant metadiscourse with multiple discourses—also advocated by the editors and contributors to *AltDis: Alternative Discourses in the Academy* (Schroeder, Fox, & Bizzell, 2004)—based on historical and cultural diversity can lead to a shift in my perceptions of a hierarchically and patriarchally ordered universe.

I see my interest in and support of feminist scholarship, and my experiences as a woman in academia as more reason to look closely at issues of power relations. Although we are supposed to think otherwise, I remain convinced that we still live in a male-dominated society where authority is often used to reinforce existing gender roles and to perpetuate an unequal distribution of social and political authority. I agree with Jane Flax (1990) when she pointed out that we need to resist the temptation to suppress "discourses that threaten to differ with or undermine the [autonomous] authority of the dominant one" (p. 48)—including discourses of women who do not share the majority's viewpoint. Instead, she sees it as necessary to "tolerate and interpret ambivalence, ambiguity, and multiplicity as well as to expose the roots of our needs for imposing order and structure no matter how arbitrary and oppressive these needs may be" (p. 56). Although I admire and agree with Flax, I have often wondered how I can move away from the structure that is imposed by academic requirements. Despite my wish to foreground ambiguity, I know that tenure and promotion committees follow strict guidelines that determine my status at the university. I also know that I have the power and authority to be ambiguous in my classrooms, but such power is part of an order that I impose on students.

What I hope to achieve in my interactions with students and colleagues is more closely based on Audre Lorde's (1990) advocacy for alternative modes of communication based on equality—using each other's differences and each other's authorities to gain new insights. As she put it:

> Our future survival is predicated upon our ability to relate within equality. As women, we must root out internalized patterns of oppression within ourselves if we are to move beyond the most superficial aspects of social change. Now we must recognize differences among women who are our equals, neither inferior nor superior, and devise ways to use each others' difference to enrich our visions and our joint struggles. (p. 286)

Audre Lorde's comments on using our differences to enrich how we see and interact with each other reminded me of Andrea Lunsford's (2000) comments in"Refiguring Classroom Authority." Instead of struggling with reinterpreting the meaning of authority, Lunsford suggested moving the discussion toward taking "responsibility for words and actions and positions in the classroom" (p. 74). I was hopeful that learning from each other and capitalizing from a variety of ideas and opinions while at the same time moving away from autonomous toward dialogic authority and toward responsibility would be an outcome of computer-mediated communication (CMC) as well. I had read early work by Emily Jessup (1991), for example, who argued for feminist scholarship in computers and composition that moves toward undermining hierarchical structures and male-dominated discourse (p. 351). I had also looked at articles by Gail Hawisher and Cynthia Selfe (1991) who, while criticizing overly enthusiastic accounts of computer use in classrooms without looking at potential problems, also stressed that "if we plan carefully and examine our integration of technology critically, computers have the potential for helping us shift traditional authority structures inherent in American education" (p. 64). However, I was also careful to listen to their cautious remarks that "although the use of computer technology may give us greater freedom to construct more effective learning environments, it may also lead us unknowingly to assume positions of power that contradict our notions of good teaching" (p. 64). In other words, unequal power relations are not dismantled by the medium used but by the implementation of the technology in a classroom setting and by the pedagogical framework that allows for dialogic instead of autonomous relations (see also Regan, 1993; Romano, 1993; Takayoshi, 1994). Recent explorations of, and reflections on, online interactions (Blair & Monske, 2003; Bomberger, 2004; de Montes et al., 2002; McKee, 2002; Sheridan-Rabideau, McLaughlin, & Novak, 2002; Smith, 2004) also confirm the need to be critical about the impact that CMC can have on student learning, making it clear that the results do not necessarily depend on the tool but rather on how the tool is implemented in an existing structure constrained by the specific circumstances under which the interactions take place. The following section provides some insights into how students addressed issues of authority in an online discussion, and how I interpreted their use of authority as part of an already existing hierarchical and patriarchal structure.

## AUTHORITY IN THE CLASSROOM: SHIFTING PERCEPTIONS

As a teacher, I am convinced that learning takes place in many ways. It does not only include reading and writing the word, but, as Freire and

Macedo (1987) said, also reading and writing the *world*. Part of reading the world and gaining a better understanding of one's subject position is engaging in discussions concerning issues that are not necessarily easy to talk about and that can lead to disagreement and to conflict. According to Beverly Daniel Tatum (1997), race, class, and gender are often especially challenging for students. As she said, "It is very difficult to talk about [race, class, and/or gender] in a meaningful way without also talking and learning about racism, classism, and sexism. The introduction of these issues of oppression often generates powerful emotional responses in students that range from guilt and shame to anger and despair. If not addressed, these emotional responses can result in student resistance to oppression-related content areas" (pp. 1-2). Rape and date rape cross race, class, and gender lines, and often lead to emotional reactions. Men might be afraid to be seen as potential perpetrators, and women might feel uncomfortable because they are trained to see themselves as partly responsible for "allowing" rape to happen. The unequal power relations between the sexes often reinforce the perception that rape is inflicted by the woman on herself. And although date rape is seen as the new student fear on college campuses (Hill, 2004), it is rarely discussed outside of special prevention workshops that are often poorly attended. Furthermore, those present at take-back-the-night rallies are mostly women and men who are already aware of the detrimental consequences of rape and date rape.

In this writing course, students participated in choosing the topics that would be used as starting points for writing response papers and writing their own argument papers. One of the topics they chose centered around discussions of date rape. According to the reader we used, discussions of this topic were intended to raise awareness of what is considered date rape, the reasons for committing date rape, various resources available for women and men to discuss ways of fighting against date rape, and to discuss fears of being labeled a rapist or being labeled an "easy woman." I had my reservations about exploring such volatile issues, but I also wanted to honor student choices in topic discussions. My main worry centered around the sensitivity of this topic, and the likelihood that one of the women had experienced sexual assault or rape and would feel uncomfortable during our discussions.

To sensitize students toward the topic, and to provide them with a variety of opportunities to think about the topic, the students were asked to "study" a wreath put up in memory of victims of rape and date rape, or, to put it in Freirean terms, to read the word and the world. Additionally, participants in this course watched a documentary in class about a university student who had experienced date rape and had, after a long silence, agreed to talk about it openly. Using a wreath and a documentary as reading material before engaging in an online discussion was intended to provide students with information that they could connect to their own lives and to their own environment. In the ideal case, this would engage them in active and critical participation. Embedding the online discussion within this context was also intended to provide students with a certain amount of authority on the topic, which they could then share with their class members and from which other participants could profit, putting the concept of dialogic authority into practice.

In discussions leading up to the online exchange, I had collected a multitude of materials that showed the detrimental effects of rape on the victims, and I had tried to predispose students to seeing rape and date rape as crimes that were perpetrated by the aggressor and that could not be blamed on the victim. I felt justified in using my authority to control the information that students received because, from my perspective, students were exposed to a multitude of negative stereotypes about women's positions in cases of rape. Additionally, a rape resulting in the murder of the victim—a university employee—and the suicide of the alleged rapist—a student at the university—shortly before the discussion took place, left me and many women on campus paralyzed. It also made me more conscious of the victimization of women, and the disempowerment that many women experienced.

My own strong feelings on this topic, I later realized, did not open up the classroom for dialogic interactions; instead, I assumed that students, based on their critical awareness and their ability to engage in productive dialogue, would react to discussions on rape and date rape similarly to how I reacted. As a woman and a feminist, I just could not fathom that anybody would question who the guilty party in rape cases was. I did not accept any arguments that tried to justify a rapist's action, and I was even less tolerant of people who were convinced that a rape victim participated and encouraged rape. From our in-class discussions, I assumed that all the students shared my perspective, but I did not realize that I might have silenced those students who did not agree with me.

Students at that time were quite familiar with using the online forum for synchronous discussions. Similar to other meetings online, they could log on from different labs on campus. Furthermore, two students from the class served as discussion leaders, taking on the responsibility of providing a dialogic environment where ideas could be shared and students could learn from each other. However, unlike the previous times, this meeting happened at the end of the semester and was not followed by a face-to-face meeting where class members could discuss the entries in the online forum and where they would have to be accountable for their online words in a face-to-face environment.

The number of responses (272), and, more importantly, the contents of the responses during the online activities, can be attributed to many factors—an explosive topic, end-of-semester mood, strong involvement with the issue, and importantly, issues of voice and authority. I do not know whether this discussion should be called a success or whether it falls in the category of failed attempt at awareness raising, maybe even leading to more extreme and less understanding positions than previously existed. I do not have an easy answer, and I am still conflicted about my role as a researcher and teacher. Could I have changed how authority was used by various class members? Could I have contributed more to establish an interactive pattern that privileged dialogic authority instead of the well-established patterns of hegemonic authority? I provide a close analysis of the discussion to show how difficult it is as a researcher, teacher, or student to understand issues of authority and to understand how we are implicated in exercising authority that does not lead to dialogue and reflection. Here, I attempt to critically appraise the existing positionalities that make it difficult to move outside any established and endorsed social, political, and educational practices and expectations.

## THEY WANT IT: A REAFFIRMATION OF LONG-HELD BELIEFS

After the initial "hi everyone," "hello out there," and "I'm here," one of the discussion leaders started the conversation with a question that she had after watching the documentary on acquaintance rape:

> I thought I would go ahead and ask a question on date rape or acquaintance rape. In the video we watched, the girl that was raped said she did not report it. This made me feel like either she was lying or she wanted it and was easy. But wait before you jump all over me; I'm not the only one in this country that feels this way. A lot of women feel the same way, what do you think? (Olivia)

Olivia posed a question that is of real concern to her and that she has problems answering. Olivia is aware that her opinion could cause some dissent. Her assertion that "a lot of women feel the same way" could be an attempt to validate her opinion. It could also be an attempt to move against the position of the teacher, who, for several class sessions, insisted that the victim cannot and should not be blamed for being raped. I showed no tolerance for any other perspective, and I countered every statement defending the rapist with what I considered strong and convincing arguments that the rapist was the one to blame.

The online responses, however, show that the participants are struggling with the definition of rape, and with the implications of not going public after acquaintance rape. Miriam, although she can understand Olivia's concerns, nevertheless disagreed:

> Olivia I see your point, but I do not think she was easy just because she kept quiet . . . maybe she knew she could not handle what might happen if the word got out . . . it might have been in her best interest. (Miriam)

Miriam defended the victim who only talked about her rape long after the incident. Carla also thinks that talking about rape could be difficult for the victim:

> I don't think that some people could handle what they might have to go through in order to report a person and bring them down. (Carla)

Carla's comment is based on the documentary's discussion on the difficulties that women encounter when they press charges against the perpetrator. Similarly, Egan takes the documentary as the basis for his answer and defended the woman:

> I don't think the girl was lying because she didn't press charges against the guy. She probably didn't want to deal with it any longer. (Egan)

I saw the comments as working toward a better understanding of what it means for a woman to go public after date rape. Olivia's initial question seemed to raise compassion for the rape victim, but did not lead to a defense of the rapist. I saw comments by Miriam, Carla, and Egan as engaging in dialogic discussions, pointing out to Olivia that it is not the victim who is at fault but that the situation itself, with all its social and cultural stigmas, creates an untenable situation for the victim. These students were engaged in the topic, and because they agreed with me, I started to applaud them in their efforts to dispel the myths about rape.

However, moving from the documentary to a more amorphous and less focused discussion on why rape occurs, the attention shifted to another student who was curious about the power relations at play in date rape situations:

> Hey you all do you think that guys only rape the girl to prove themselves to their friends? (Masad)

Masad's question is taken up by a number of the participants whose opinions differ widely:

> NO, I feel that most rapes occur because women put themselves in situations where they lead a man to the point where he won't take no for an answer. (Bailey)

> Masad, not all the time but I think it has a lot to do with wanting someone or something real bad and not wanting to take no for and answer. (Carla)

> Masad, I don't think that is always true, but probably a lot of the time. (Josi)

> I agree with Bailey, if you don't want a person to get the wrong impression, let them know where you stand. I would [rather] want to hurt a person's feelings than get raped. (Ricardo)

> Masad: No. I feel that miscommunication and consequently bad judgment are the cause of all date rape. Women and men need to let the person know up front what they are after. When men are b.s'ng about how they feel they end up taking drastic measures to get what they want. Also, when women are teasing and not showing how they really feel, they end up getting hurt. People need to let people know what they want and stop beating around the bush. (Langston)

> I think that rape is like this whole power trip...maybe they feel in command? It's sick. (Miriam)

> Just because a woman lets a guy know what her feelings are and what she does or does not want to do, she still has a chance of being attacked or forced into doing something (Carla)

These comments show a marked shift from the initial responses to Olivia's question. Now, instead of seeing the woman as the one who gets hurt most, Bailey, Ricardo, and Langston see her as the one responsible for male advances. Miriam's and Carla's voices seem to disappear in this exchange; instead, Bailey comments that women need to be more straightforward when interacting with men:

> I believe that sometimes women get to a point where they feel that they are obligated in having sex for whatever reasons. After the fact these women feel as though their rights have been infringed upon, therefore justify their actions by calling rape. (Bailey)

John agreed with Bailey:

> I agree with Bailey I think sometimes women allow themselves to be talked into doing something they didn't really want to and then call it rape the next day. (John)

When I read these comments, my belief in my abilities to raise critical awareness about social, political, economic, and cultural inequalities failed. I knew that these views were not only defended by participants of this online session but, as Deborah L. Siegel (1992) pointed out in her work on sexual harassment, they were shared by many people who often blame the woman for being raped. However, I had firmly believed that our previous discussions had dispelled what I considered sexist and unfounded opinions. At that time, I didn't reflect on my own role in suppressing controversial beliefs, and my inability to accept that my students would bring their own contextualized perspectives to the discussion.

I started to realize that some of the male students took the discussion very personally and had most likely considered themselves outnumbered during in-class discussions. For example, Bailey seemed to fear that he could be considered a potential perpetrator. He expressed this ambiguity in one of his messages after Olivia had pointed out that "no means no and yes means yes":

> No means No and yes means yes to a certain point. I have been in many situations where I have been told no but upon further actions ends up leading to having sex, so does this mean that I'm a rapist, after all she said no. (Bailey)

I was surprised that nobody in the class responded directly to this question. The discussion, although heated and controversial, seemed to avoid the dangerous territory of personal experiences, despite Bailey's effort to provoke a comment about his own behavior. Instead, students focused on other parts of the exchange, seemingly evading a possibly volatile exchange. Bailey's authority in this case seems to be based on his personal knowledge that it is not easy to know whether a woman really doesn't want to have sex. It is an authority based on his beliefs concerning the roles of women and men. His authority appears to be legitimized by other class members who expressed similar opinions. However, most of the other participants discussed the topic as largely unconnected to their own lives, keeping a safe distance that allows them to talk abstractly about their position on acquaintance rape. When one of the participants asked whether anybody knew a rape victim, the initial unanimous answer of those responding was "no," removing any form of close personal involvement from the topic discussed. This separation of other and self is also obvious in the following examples. What I found interesting—but no longer surprising—in these responses by the male participants in the exchange is the almost exclusive emphasis on the role and responsibilities of women:

> Part of a woman's responsibility is to be aware. Know who you are dating; is he a jerk, have you heard any stories of him. Don't make yourself susceptible; going to his apartment, car, room, or anyplace where no one is around. (Eric)

> I think alcohol is an important factor when it comes to women thinking they were raped. They may say yes that night and wake up and not remember a thing. She knows what probably happened and realizes that she didn't want to have sex so she will cry rape. (Jay)

> I feel that women shouldn't allow themselves in that type of situation because they are the ones that are getting raped all the time. If men were getting raped all the time, they shouldn't let themselves get in that situation. (Alex)

> I feel that more women should get the picture on how rape can be interpreted many different ways and understand that rape is hard to prove under most circumstances. Since rape is such a hard thing to prove then women should take it upon themselves to stay away from unfavorable conditions. (Bailey)

Repeatedly, women—as abstract human beings and not necessarily close friends or members of this class—are made responsible for recognizing and avoiding the potential dangers they are prone to encounter in various dating situations. When I reread the responses, I found it useful to relate comments by Eric, Jay, Alex, and Bailey to their own socialization and experiences in what I assumed to be a largely traditional and patriarchal environment. It seemed easy for them to objectify women and diminish the role of men in sexual harassment and rape cases. Other members of the class also voiced their opinions during this exchange, but like Eric, Jay, Alex, and Bailey, they too seemed to contribute to the "authoritarian" exchange that did not encourage women's participation but instead sidelined them and contributed more to their victimization. Dialogue did not seem a possibility, opinions were clearly delineated, and women's voices were mostly left out of the conversation.

Of course, I can now wonder how I was implicated in this exchange. Was it my lack of wonder, to use Iris Marion Young's (1997) words, in how the men in the class would react to and understand discussions on rape? In some ways, I assumed symmetrical reciprocity, insisting that no matter who we are, rape would be considered the fault of the perpetrator. I was not curious to learn about other perspectives, and I did not respect other worldviews. I can't say that even to this day I respect the perspectives brought to my attention by students like Eric, Jay, Alex, and Bailey, but I am now more aware that I need to find out more about how students, colleagues, or administrators come by their specific opinions. I found that only when I know more about others is it possible to negotiate and come to an understanding of how I am influenced by who I work with, how my own belief systems hamper my interactions in political, social, or educational settings, and why I don't accept certain viewpoints in those with whom I interact professionally or personally.

## IT COULD BE YOU: BRINGING THE DISCUSSION BACK HOME

I painted a bleak picture of some of my students' discouraging discourse strategies. But despite my despondency about the direction of the discussion, and despite my concerns about my own participation in how students interacted and responded, it seemed that some students were willing to bring the discussion closer to home and to address some of the generalizing comments made during the exchange. Alba decided that she wanted to post a message in response to Bailey's comments. The message takes him to task on what Alba considers an unwarranted appropriation of the dominant discourse:

> Bailey? If women regret sex they will call it rape?
>
> Look unless you know that for a fact, that is a very strong comment to make. Why would a woman want to put herself through that? I've seen trial proceedings on rape cases and the defendant's strategy is always to portray the woman as a slut "who asked for it." I don't know about anyone else but I'm sure I would rather just deal with regret, than have someone come out and try to portray me as a slut with no credibility as a human being! (Alba)

Based on my own worldview, I saw this message as an attempt to bring the discussion back to the issue at hand: the detrimental effects of rape on women's dignity, self-esteem, health, education, and so on. I hoped that other students would join in and support Alba's comments. I was pleased, and my own beliefs on the subject were reaffirmed, when Olivia responded on a more personal level:

> Alba, I agree! But if I got raped I would go to hell and back to make sure this guy got what he deserves. (Olivia)

Here, Alba and Olivia were able to express their concerns with becoming rape victims and at the same time, they questioned the authority assumed by Eric, Bailey, Alex, and Jay. After her first message as a moderator that questioned the sincerity of the woman raped on campus, Olivia shifted her focus and seemed to work actively to challenge comments that contributed to stereotyping the rape victim. A very pointed query that I posted, and one that left little doubt about how I felt—after a discussion that Carla and Olivia had about women who "agree" to have sex with multiple partners—also elicited some personal responses:

> Carla and Olivia, but what if she wasn't given an option? What if she was forced to have sex? Raped? Over and over again. (Sibylle)
>
> Sibylle I can't even answer that question. It makes me feel so bad to even thing that I could have something so precious to me taken away

> by force. I would most definitely go to hell and back to see that he suffer! (Olivia)
>
> Sibylle, If that happened to me I would feel so bashed up, used and hurt that I don't think I could keep something of that magnitude inside for a long period of time at all. On the other hand, if alcohol or anything else had been involved, then I couldn't help myself but to think that is way partially my fault also. (Carla)

These comments indicated to me the strong feelings that the topic elicited from Olivia and Carla. But I also recognized that I left little room for any disagreement when I posted my question. I used my authority to make sure that I would get the responses I was looking for and Olivia took an aggressive stance and pledged to punish anybody who violated her body. Although Carla agreed with Olivia's comments, she showed some uncertainty about her position in the case of intoxication. Her comment led to a further exchange, eliciting responses and questions from other participants. Masad, for example, wanted to know whether Carla would blame herself if alcohol were involved:

> Carla Are you saying that if you were drinking and accidentally led the guy on. Then you would think that it is partially your fault. (Masad)

Carla responded to Masad's query and also received a response back:

> Masad, only if I didn't want it and I had said no but it still continued to happen. You start second guessing yourself and you start to think that maybe it was your fault afterall. (Carla)
>
> But Carla it is not your fault. You shouldn't second guess yourself. If you were in control of your actions and specifically said no then it is a no. (Masad)

I tried to approach this very hotly debated topic by pointing out that intoxication is no justification for abuse:

> Carla, I think that your reactions are shared by a lot of women, but I think that even if alcohol is involved, it doesn't mean that somebody can violate my body and have sex without me agreeing to do so. Of course, it's not a clear-cut issue. If I said yes, out of free will, I would

> not say I was raped afterwards, but if I do not agree to have sex, I would consider that rape. (Sibylle)

During these exchanges, the comments no longer centered around the question of who is to blame but on how complicated it is to discuss such a volatile topic and how many aspects have to be considered before forming an opinion. I don't know whether Carla and Olivia would have expressed the same opinions if the question I asked of them had been less partial. I also don't know whether my comments on alcohol consumption and involuntary sex left any room for further comments. At that time, I didn't see my comments as particularly powerful, and I didn't see myself as part of the "triangular formations of power and knowledge with the expert at the apex and the 'masses' at the base" (Hebdige, 1979, p. 226). I saw myself more closely aligned to what Mortensen and Kirsch (1993) viewed as a model of authority based on "dialogue, connectedness, and contextual rules" (p. 557). But I do have to consider my role as the teacher, albeit this role was less apparent in an online discussion. In other words, did my authority push the discussion in the direction I thought most productive, or would the discussion have encompassed these opinions without my interference?

My reflection on my own authority, however, becomes mute when considering that the exchange just presented lasted only for a short interval and did not get addressed later in the discussion. What followed instead were declarative statements that did not call for a response but instead, as illustrated in the following comments, were attacks geared toward one person, or a defense of a given statement.

> I [am] really disappointed to say that some women do agree to having sex with various partners or while others watched. But in this case it was just girls. I was 12 years old the first time I heard about it. This was around the time everyone I used to play kick the can with was growing into their own thing. We were all the same age. I stayed a tomboy, but some of my friends kept hanging around the boys for different reasons. The boys got into gangs. I guess the girls still wanted to hang on to our childhood friendship so they allowed themselves at 12 years old to be gang raped. Or rather to have the "train pulled on them." You know that really wasn't the half of it though, the boys taped it, and it took place on an old smelly matress in an abandoned house. You lose your self-respect as a person like that. I don't totally fault the girls, they didn't know any better. But you would think someone out of the group would have respect enough for a woman to say it was wrong. But no one cared—it was good entertainment just like at the frat parties in the video. There is really no difference between the incidents. They are

both "gangs, and were good entertainment" and most importantly someone was hurt for the rest of their lives. One less woman will stand proud of who she is, because maybe she didn't have enough respect for herself and no one else did either. It's in a way the fault of everyone there for not caring enough. (Alba)

Alba, in that case I blame the parents for not giving those children any morals. (Bailey)

Bailey isn't date rape a moral issue anyway. (Olivia)

Bailey, because some one is a rapist or raped doesn't mean they don't have morals. A rapist can be a well educated man [or] on ignorant one. (Olivia)

Morals are another part of rape. Hopefully most of our parents taught us whats wrong and whats right. (Eric)

Olivia, I commented on what Alba said and that situation was not date rape. (Bailey)

By this time and age I believe that parents have heard enough horror stories and rape and sex and how kids are starting to have sex at an earlier and earlier stage. Whether the parents think it is appropriate or not to discuss things like this at a young age I think it is time that they look at the big picture and what's happening. They need to teach their children moral for the sake of their lives. (Carla)

OK Bailey. Rape in general? Alba you can come in at anytime. (Olivia)

Bailey, I know their parents. That's not the case. See we all grew up in the same environment. We all could of gone either way. I could of been a mother of three with an addiction to crack. Afterall, that's what i've been exposed to all my life why not follow the trend. My point is regardless of your moral background, there are other influences (society) that have alot to do with it. (Alba)

Alba: Is it gang rape if the girls allowed themselves to do that? (Langston)

> Langston, they were 12 years old. She consented to sex to only one of them. I said she allowed herself because she couldn't do anything but take it. It was rape. (Alba)
>
> Society, doesn't instill moral values, your parents do, we all have choices to make sometimes in our lives, based on our moral values we make the right or wrong decision. I know we all make mistakes but in that situation Alba, it all starts at home. (Bailey)
>
> Alba: She couldn't just go home, huh? (Langston)
>
> She lived right next door. They lived right next door. Let me just say that these questions are a good reflection of what a victim would have to go through, defend her actions. Besides she consented to only one boy the others just joined in, and she didn't or couldn't refuse. (Alba)
>
> Alba: I think it's more of she didn't rather than she couldn't. (Langston)
>
> Alba, what do you mean she couldn't refuse? If she would have refused then she would have had a case but since she didn't, END OF STORY. (Bailey)

Alba's initial posting elicited a large number of responses. However, the discussion was mostly confrontational and, if the same discussion had been conducted face to face, might have ended up as a shouting match. As Alba pointed out, the pervading attitude was one of putting the blame on the victim, and once that had been said, it was supposed to be the "end of the story," precluding any additional comments on the topic.

When I looked back at the transcript, I saw the exchange as an unfortunate validation of many long-established and sanctioned beliefs, reaffirming Andrea Lunsford's (2000) comment that dialogic authority cannot be achieved without uncovering "the silent supports of traditional authority" (p. 76). I made assumptions about my students' and my own positions in this discussion, hoping that students would take responsibility in ways that conformed to my perception of productive classroom discussions. Instead, what I saw was a shift from taking responsibility to blaming society at large. "Morals" became an important part in understanding the direction of the discussion. Morals, or the absence of morals, seemingly account for most of the problems with American society. Similar to the emphasis on morals in the 2004 presidential elections, Bailey seemed to insist that if parents had instilled morals in their children, rape would not happen. This means, to take Bailey's comment to its logical conclusion, that the girls, as well as the boys, are immoral human beings, and that it is the parents' fault that their daughter was raped and that their sons are rapists. Olivia made an interesting connection between morals and education. It seems to be the educated people who have higher moral values than those who are not educated. Alba knows that it's not that simple because she knew the parents, but her efforts to complicate the situation and to bring in the impact of societal forces were largely ignored.

When I analyzed this exchange, I knew that my predilections and ideologies, to refer to Min-Zhan Lu's (1999) commentary on critical affirmation, played a major part in how I reacted to and interpreted the comments. I have considered myself a feminist for many years, a postmodernist for most of my adult life, and a believer in a student-centered classroom for most of my teaching life. I did not know the terms that labeled my beliefs and my actions until I went to college, but I probably would have been considered outside the norm of gender behavior in my hometown. My parents called it rebellious, unruly, disobedient, and unbecoming to a 5-year-old girl who should be interested in dressing up and playing house. Instead, I decided that it was more interesting to run around with my brothers, get muddy and dirty, and use a hammer that landed squarely on my finger. I don't know if I would argue that I was a 5-year-old feminist instead of a little terror to my parents, but I do know that my early experiences influenced my later understanding of what it meant to be a feminist.

I interpreted the responses to Alba's comments based on my predilections as a firm believer in women's equal rights and opportunities. I did not know much about Alba's background at that time, and I could only imagine how hard it must have been for her to post the extended entry. In class, I might have mentioned my own experiences with sexual harassment, but these experiences were minor in comparison to what Alba described. I also realized that I could not steer the discussion into a less volatile and—from my perspective—more productive direction. I could not take control, nor could I establish my authority—based on my role as the teacher, based on dialogic interactions, or based on my responsibility to my students—to move the discussion away from blaming the victim.

## BLAMING THE VICTIM: MYTHS REVISITED

Although Bailey apparently wanted to put a closure to this interchange, it wasn't the end of the story. Despite the apparently accusing comments from a number of participants, Alba decided to continue the discussion, and instead of being silenced, the persisting attacks prompted her to talk not only about her friend, but also about herself:

> See you guys are getting into wording; everything I say is being pecked at. It was rape damn it!
>
> I never really said anything about my encounter but since we are on the topic and I'm getting kind of frustrated. I attended a party a couple of years back. I went with a really good friend of mine. I started drinking what he thought was liqour, but really pop. He waited a while and all the while telling me to drink more. He said we were going to leave and that he had parked the car somewhere else, we started walking off somewhere weird. I got scared and started to turn back. He grabbed, put me up against the side of a house and tried to force himself on me. I struggled for a bit but thank God a car came around. I wasn't raped, but if I was and wanted to press charges, is it my fault for walking off with someone I've known and thought I was my friend. (Alba)

This courageous self-exposure seemed to be Alba's attempt to continue the exchange and to provide more examples why the opinions, especially those of Bailey and Langston, unjustly blamed the victim. This could be considered dialogic interaction on Alba's part, establishing her authority and seeing her engaged and also empowered. She was able to express herself, to engage in literate behavior that questions current oppressive behaviors, but despite a few encouraging comments from some of her peers (Miriam, Olivia, Carla, Josi, and Egan) and her instructor, her approach to authority was not reciprocated by most of the group.

Instead of working toward a rethinking of preconceived notions, some participants continued their confrontational stance toward rape victims. Alex's and Langston's first reaction was not characterized by compassion, understanding, or a rethinking of homogeneous power structures, but they partly accused Alba of having left out information about her behavior during the incident:

> Are you telling the whole story Alba? (Alex)

> Alba: Is that EVERYTHING that happened? You didn't lead him on and you didn't know his intentions right? (Langston)

Langston continued his interrogation by arguing that he wanted to know both sides of the story, thus devaluing Alba's comment as unreliable:

> Alba: Did you know his intentions? I'm not picking on you, I'm just being fair to both sides. (Langston)

These comments clearly moved away from the concept of electronic communication as "safe space." What complicated these interactive patterns even more is that Alex and Langston not only talked online, but because they were in the same location, they first commented on the postings offline before they wrote online. They were both very indignant about Alba's posting and reinforced each other in the belief that she was hiding parts of the story to put herself in a positive light. I was the only other person in the same room with them but did not get involved in their discussion because I did not want to exercise "instructor authority." Now I am not sure whether I should have used my own privileged position—my authority of office—to address how their comments might be perceived and what their comments might achieve. However, I did not confront Alex and Langston; instead, I was hoping, however naively, that conflict and struggle would lead to increased critical awareness.

Although Alba did find a space that allowed her to write a lengthy post, discourse was mostly based on interactive strategies that I saw as following a hierarchical and nondialogic pattern. Bailey continued this pattern—which was later on picked up by John—by moving away from the act of near-rape itself and by emphasizing the level of nonintoxication of Alba instead:

> Alba, you were lucky, but should you have told him you were drinking pop and he wouldn't have tried to force himself upon you. You would have had a viable argument because you didn't give consent, But your friend didn't say no. (Bailey)

> Alba, I agree with Bailey if you had told him you were drinking pop then the whole situation could have been avoided. (John)

With these comments, Alba was blamed for *not* being drunk and thus leading on the person who was claiming he would take her home. The participants in the class followed closely the three myths that Deborah L. Siegel (1992) pointed out in her work on sexual harassment and rape.

1. Women ask for it: Victims "seduce" their rapists.
2. Women say no but mean yes: Women secretly need and want to be forced into sex. They don't know what they want.
3. Women lie: In most charges of "rape," the woman is lying. (pp. 150-151)

Repeatedly, Alba's authority was undermined by the participants, and she was put into a situation where her experiences were reconstructed as unreliable, and, even more drastically, as partly fabricated. In this part of the exchange, her voice was ignored, and she became the subject of a number of attacks from her peers. Thus, although online discussions allowed for more voices than face-to-face discourse usually does, the nature of discourse in electronic communication was not necessarily discourse that endorsed Faigley's (1992) concept of "centrifugal forces of multiplicity, equality, and uncertainty" (p. 183). Instead, this part of the discussion relied on dominant discourse strategies that endorsed unequal power relations, and it did not achieve dialogic action and equality among the students. It became what Faigley seems to connect mostly to face-to-face discussions where "monologic centripetal forces of unity, authority, and truth" (p. 183) determine the relationships between students and between students and the instructor.

In an attempt to support Alba and to challenge some of the responses, Olivia took Alex to task for what she considered an insinuating question. Langston also joined the exchange:

> Alex that is so ugly of you to ask such a question! I can't believe you would even [do that]! (Olivia)
>
> That is not an ugly question because maybe she didn't want to reveal some things to us. (Alex)
>
> Like what more is their to reveal Alex, that some jerk tried to get a quickie and leave? (Olivia)
>
> There could be more. Look at the boy's point of view. (Alex)

> Olivia: The man's not here to defend himself so we have only what Alba SAYS to believe. (Langston)

Olivia's efforts in defending Alba did not lead to the responses she might have hoped for, nor did it lead to responses that moved away from criticizing Alba's actions. Instead, in addition to discounting her experience, Alba is dismissed as a person, and the comments are no longer addressed to her. She is instead referred to in the third person without having her presence online acknowledged. It almost seems that the absence of a physical presence influenced the reactions here. Because Olivia, Alex, and Langston could not see Alba, they did not seem to perceive her as a major part of the exchange. Alba's objectification, her temporarily being "written out of the story," further problematized the shifting nature of power dynamics online. Although power did shift from the instructor to some of the students, it did not lead to the elimination of domination; instead, for Alba, it led to domination by elimination.

The instructor, in this exchange, similar to other unheard voices, went unnoticed for the most part. The response to student reactions was rather pointed, but because other exchanges were going on at the same time, it had little impact on the class members:

> I can't believe the reactions to Alba's story. Unfortunately, I think that's the reaction of a large part of the population, an ugly reaction nevertheless. It's completely beside the point whether Alba was drinking pop or alcohol—my God, somebody wanted to rape her, that's the point! (Sibylle)

Because my role was configured as "participant"—a role that I occupied during the previous online discussions as well—I responded as a participant who very clearly disagreed with the opinions voiced by Bailey, Langston, and Alex. Here, a student in my own classroom—as Faigley would call it—I had little influence over the direction of the conversation. Although a shift from autonomous authority to multiple authorities in dialogue with each other is a desirable goal in any setting, the relinquishing of authority in order to build a new but equally restricting authority did not serve the purpose of a cooperative, heterogeneous, and collaborative classroom. Furthermore, becoming a student in my own class is not necessarily the best expression for my situation. I would argue that my role as the instructor was present in all online discussions, but that through negotiation my role as an instructor was redefined and included a cooperative and collaborative aspect that shifted the power relationships in the classroom and allowed for student-centered interactions. I remember wanting to protect Alba and save her from the comments, only I didn't know how—I had no power, no authority, could not dominate the discussion because I was only one voice among many voices. I very consciously did not ask them to stop the discussion because I had promised my students not to take on the role of the discussion leader. Re-reading the comments, I don't know if that caused more harm than it did good. Additionally, I don't know if it would even have been possible to stop the discussion in the first place.

Alba's move from a subject to an object position, from speaking for herself to being spoken about, was again reversed toward the end of the exchange. Alba once more tried to articulate her anger about the direction of the discussion:

> Again. Did you lead him on? What were you wearing? Is it the whole story? Thousands of women don't want to say anything because they don't want to be grilled. NO, NO NO, NO, I said no stop!
>
> He said we were going home. That's the whole story. No wait I ran to the party and went home with someone else. And you know what he stayed it turns out to get what he didn't get off of me from three other girls. (Alba)

In this entry, Alba related her situation to the situation of "thousands of women" who, if they went public and denounced the perpetrator, run the risk of encountering comments that put the blame on them. She very quickly, however, shifted the focus and defended her behavior during the near-rape to counter the accusations but also to show her anger with the attitude of those accusing her. Alba's posting received one compassionate response:

> Alba, I can't believe that some of these people in this classroom can be so insensitive. I have never been raped but I can imagine what you've been going through. (Olivia)

None of the other participants continued the discussion, but instead had already logged off or were in the process of logging off. The final comment, however, and the last word, was Alba's:

> See you all. Merry Christmas! Olivia it's only made me as a woman stronger and work harder for what I believe in. (Alba)

Apparently, Alba could distance herself from the comments made during the online discussion, and the accusations brought against her did not defeat her belief in herself. This, however, did not erase the fact that the online exchanges followed a pattern that built on dominant discourses instead of disrupting them.

## IS THERE HOPE? SYNCHRONOUS AND ASYNCHRONOUS EXCHANGES

One hour and 15 minutes seemed enough to shatter my belief in the practicality of critical pedagogy, dialogic authority, and social awareness in online discussions. The hostility in parts of the transcript overshadowed the whole discussion, and although some exchanges were fruitful and did lead to thoughtful comments, the apparent lack of respect for rape victims exhibited by some participants took on singular significance for me. I would have given in to my existentialist despair had it not been for another discussion strand. Fortunately, in addition to the synchronous discussion on acquaintance rape, students had gone to the patio in the Student Union and had watched a documentary on date rape, and they discussed their impressions online throughout the week. Some students posted before the synchronous discussion, some during it, but most of them posted after the discussion.

Similar to the synchronous discussion, opinions varied; however, the postings on this forum were much less aggressive and confrontational, and they also showed more complex approaches to the topic. Thus, although many of the male participants attached some of the blame to a rape victim's behavior, they also acknowledged that rape is a serious problem.

> The wreath in the Illini Union to me seemed to represent more than just those women who feel as though they have been sexually assaulted. I got the feeling that it represented all women in that today women are beginning to take a stand and letting men know that women are no longer going to be the quiet, innocent victim anymore. To me sexual assault can be interpreted many different ways, so I feel as though sometimes women have an advantage in such cases because any women can claim that they have been assaulted even if they went along with the actions that took place. In most cases of sexual assault people tend to take the side of the victim even if her claim is false so

> the man in the situation in some cases is already guilty by just the claim alone. (Bailey)

> Rape is a serious problem. In the video we watched in class the girl didn't press charges. I think that she should have pressed charges. I think that anyone that is raped should press charges, confronting the person who raped you is not enough. In the video it said one out of three girls on this campus is raped and on the wreath in the Patio it says one out of six girls is raped on this campus. Both numbers are high, but I think that some of those cases shouldn't be considered rape. I think that sometimes girls regret having sex and they call it rape. When women say no men should listen to them. (Egan)

> This is about the rape issue on this campus. Walking in the patio and looking at that wreath caused me to express a feeling of anger and saddness. I can't believe that one out of every six women are getting raped or sexually abused by men they know. It is a sad thing that with so much measures and programs sponsered to stop this crime are not working. The issue of date rape is causing many women to be aware of this horrible crime. I think that men and women should be able to understand when someone means "no". I don't think that you can blame the guy always for the crime. It can partially be the girls fault too. Everyone has to understand that rape is a terrible crime and we all should help stop it. (Masad)

These entries no longer assume absolute authority on the issue but reflect the complexity of issues involved in sexual assault. Looking at the subject position—that of young men on a college campus with a high number of acquaintance rapes—these comments have to be seen as an effort in trying to understand women's positions, while at the same time defending men's positions.

The women posting to this asynchronous discussion took a different approach to date rape. Quite understandably, they did not feel a need to defend men and instead focused on the position of women. Miriam, for example, used her position as a young woman on a college campus as the starting point for expressing her concerns:

> I was in awe when I saw the documentary in class on Tuesday. I guess I never really realized that stuff like that could happen on this campus. I mean I know that it can happen, but it just seemed like it could not happen here . . . it sort of opened my eyes. I agree with Bailey about the wreath . . . it does symbolize women and it did seem to state that

> women are NOT going to be quiet about sexual assault anymore..in a way when I looked at the wreath I got a good feeling and yet a sad one also. Good because these women are not keeping quiet anymore and yet sad, because it is a shame that we even need to symbolize this issue . . . if it just did not happen at all it would not even be an issue. Rape is scary, and being a young women as myself it scares me more having seen and read about all of this stuff in the past couple of days. I can hope and pray that the sick people of this world reform there ways . . . and soon. (Miriam)

Olivia occupied a similar subject position to that of Miriam's; however, her reactions to sexual assault were less clear-cut:

> Date rape is a serious problem as well as rape. When women don't report these things they become somewhat "expected."
>
> I really don't know what I would do if this happened to me. I would just have to pray and have the support of my family and friend to deal with the entire situation. I can't help by to think that these girls got what they derserved and that the asked for it and that is so horrible of me. I hope that I can become more educated on the issue and learn what types of things occur before and after rape so I can be more aware and maybe help those that had this done to them. (Olivia)

Olivia posted her message during the synchronous discussion—before Alba posted her message on her near-rape. She admitted her conflicting beliefs, and although she knew that to accuse rape victims of bringing it on themselves "is so horrible for [her]," her cultural and social upbringing has taught her to blame the victim. However, she continued her posting later and pointed out that she wanted to increase her knowledge about rape. And, as an entry after the synchronous discussion showed, Olivia thought about it some more, and she came to the following conclusion:

> I want to comment on the situation with Alba. I think it was really brave of her to say what she had to say about her near experience with rape. Why do people have to be so insensitive? It is enough that he wanted to take advantage of her because he thought she was drunk! I have totally changed my views on this matter because by the comments that SOME individuals made on the issue made me realize that they are NOT the only ones that feel this way!! It is a cold and harsh world out there and to think that even I can judge something that I have never experienced before makes my stomach quarrel at the

> thought. Alba, If you just to happen to stop by the computer and log on I want to say good luck and have a Merry Christmas and a Happy New Year! (Olivia)

Olivia's change of attitude toward rape victims was an example of what Freire (1968) would consider "consciousness raising." In this instance, Olivia engaged in "authentic thinking," which Freire defines as "thinking that is concerned about *reality*" and which can only be achieved through communication (p. 64). In other words, the online exchange, her disenchantment with participants who blamed Alba, and her compassion for Alba provided her with the incentive to reconsider her own reality and adjust it to a new, less judgmental perception of reality.

Faigley (1992) asserted that "implications of postmodern theory for the networked classroom do not stop with giving voice to difference, decentering the authority of the teacher, or with demonstrating the social construction of knowledge" (p. 190). He used Lyotard's expression of "legitimation crisis" to argue that "there is no external authority to which we can appeal nor any way we can establish enduring values" (p. 190). This legitimation crisis, and the negation of authority and values, I found out, does not automatically negate dominant structures. Instead, different but similarly confining structures are recreated from old structures and adapted for exercising control. In other words, although some of the online exchanges provided a starting point for dialogic interaction and dialogic authority, others reverted to authoritarian discourse patterns that did not enhance communication or immediately increase students' social awareness. The wide range and often contradictory interactive behavior should not have come as a surprise (or appalling reality) to me. I know that online interaction, similar to any other kind of interaction, is influenced by a variety of factors. Participants' reactions online are determined by their subject positions, and their use of authority—autonomous or dialogic—is based on years of socialization in a hierarchical, patriarchal, and for some an oppressive environment. I had to remind myself, as Kristine Blair and Elizabeth Monske (2003) said in a recent piece on discussions of empowerment and disempowerment in online environments, that "the extent to which such networks are empowering is in fact context-based, requiring analyses of pedagogies, ideologies, and student and teacher subjectivities—and recognition that these variables, as part of any action or teacher-research methodology, are often not generalizable to every electronic learning environment" (p. 449). I also needed to remind myself that electronic communication is not the reason for student online behavior; instead, it is a powerful *tool* that can be used to dominate, liberate, control, create borders, break down borders, and keep the status quo. And since "consensus is at times politically desirable" (Faigley, 1992, p. 199), it is up to me to find ways of working toward an environment that is less conducive to domination and oppression and that strives for dialogic action based on cooperation and caring.

My reflections in this chapter have prompted me to take seriously Andrea Lunsford's (2000) call for "uncovering the silent supports of traditional authority" (p. 76) through "disrupting exclusive and exclusionary constructions of authority" and, most importantly, "we have to be committed . . . to giving up, to sharing privileges, even if it *doesn't work*" (p. 76). This online discussion did not work the way I had envisioned it, but I need to remind myself that it possibly could work, even if it might take many revisions, much rethinking, and much work on everybody's part.

The next chapter looks closely at two individuals who live within an environment where technology, as a tool, was and is often used to control, create borders, and impose authority. But the participants in this study also point out that the tool, and the appropriate implementation and contextualization of the tool, can be used to provide a better understanding of the multiple ways in which technological literacy—functional and critical—can break down borders and can become a means for preserving culture and teaching students about specific customs and languages.

# 6

# CONTEXTUALIZING LITERACIES

## TRADITIONS, CULTURES, IDENTITIES, AND TECHNOLOGIES

When I started to teach at my current institution in the American southwest, I realized early on that I needed to think about my subjectivities, that I needed to re-examine and rekindle my sense of wonder (Young, 1997). I realized that I needed to revise and expand my approach to literacy acquisition and practices, and, importantly, I needed to learn more about the literacies of Native-American groups. At my previous institution, I worked with culturally and ethnically diverse first-year students such as Alba, Celie, Bailey, Langston, Olivia, Carla, Masad, and Egan, but I had little experience with Native-American students. My PhD was from a school that sported Chief Illini, a controversial mascot performing the Chief Illini dance and printed on many alumni shirts, pens, mugs, and decals. Before I interviewed for my current job, I read that one of the goals at Northern Arizona University (NAU) was—and still is—"to be the nation's leading non-tribal university in affording educational opportunities for Native-American students, in providing service and applied research to Native-American tribes, and in advancing research concerning the history, culture, and contemporary issues of Native-American people" (NAU Mission Statement). Unlike at many other college campuses around the nation where the Native-American student population stagnates around 1%, Native-American students at NAU comprise approximately 9% percent of the overall student population (2005) with 46 tribes represented among them. The largest number are Navajos (approximately 70%), followed by Hopis (approximately 5%), and White Mountain Apaches (approximately 2%). Students might have grown up on the reservation, in rural areas, in nearby towns, or in large metropolitan areas. In other words, their educational, cultural, and economic backgrounds vary largely. Additionally, technological use differs widely, depending on access to computers, purpose for using computers, and value put on functional and critical computer literacy.

In this chapter, then, I am especially interested in exploring individuals' technological literacy acquisition and their approach to technological literacy. I was motivated by my goal as a professional educator to find out how we can successfully incorporate what we learn from individuals into our classroom teaching. In this case, the participants in this study are Navajo, which have been traditionally marginalized in the United States. Similar to Selfe and Hawisher (2004) in *Literate Lives in the Information Age*, I examine how specific social, political, cultural, historical, and economic backgrounds can help, hinder, encourage, discourage, persuade, or dissuade individuals from exploring technological literacies and from participating in the so-called technology revolution. Unlike in my other chapters, I am more interested here in an overall picture that does not involve specific classroom interactions but that lets us see the progression of literate behaviors in two women—Jolita and Mani—who were born and grew up in the Navajo Nation and who have started to explore the uses of new information technologies for educational purposes.

The framework I use for telling and analyzing Jolita's and Mani's stories is again determined by my understanding of how literacy functions based on contextual and situation specific circumstances. It situates my own literacy experiences and those of Jolita and Mani within the larger debate on how we approach literacy acquisition and literate behaviors. I also found it necessary to situate this study within Navajo Nation history and Navajo Nation education. Jolita's and Mani's experiences are the experiences of members of a tribal group living on the reservation and of individuals who participate to a larger or lesser degree in the traditions and practices of their culture and the cultures surrounding them. What I try to show is that Jolita's and Mani's technological literacies are literacies that grow out of the many other literacies that are part of their lives. They are members of a marginalized group as well as individuals whose literacies are changing constantly, adjusting to new experiences and revising old ones. This, then, is an effort to show what provides motivation for literacy acquisition, and how technologies can help or hinder this process.

## AN EDUCATIONAL JOURNEY

I was reminded during my discussions with Jolita and Mani and after looking back at my work in this chapter, that I contextualize my approaches to technological literacies within my own experiences, histories, and cultural values, and within the experiences, histories, and cultural values of those I ask to participate in my studies. I knew that if I wanted to be successful in helping NAU achieve its goal of affording "educational opportunities for Native-American students," and if I wanted to learn more about the many complexities of Native-American identity construction, I needed to find out about the social, political, economic, and educational histories connected with specific Native-American tribes. I am glad I had not read Malea Powell's (2002) comments in "Listening to Ghosts," or I might have been more reluctant to increase my understanding and knowledge of Native-American cultures. In her eyes, I might have been a "white-lady-who-loves-Indians" (p. 13), and I am not sure how I would have responded to such a comment at that time. I might have shied away from learning more, or I might have resisted such labeling by simply pointing out that I didn't love Indians, African Americans, Anglos, or Latinos. Indeed, I wasn't much taken by Americans in general, but I learned to learn more about individuals from the United States with whom I had very little in common. It helped me appreciate differences in cultures, histories, lifestyles, and especially politics. I was glad to read Lani Guinier's (Guinier & Torres, 2003) comments in *The Miner's Canary: Enlisting Race, Resisting Power, Transforming Democracy* where she pointed out the following:

> If we think in categories, and think about race only as if it were a single category, we conflate many different spheres of racial meaning. We fail to specify if we mean biological race, political race, historical race, or cultural race. We simplify race as a fixed category from which many people want to escape. They seek exit, not acknowledgement: they want choice, not voice. The category becomes a barrier, a fenced enclosure, and transgressing the boundary becomes an act of rebellion and self-definition. These negative aspects of race do not stand in for the entire experience of being "raced." (p. 4)

I started at my current institution in 1996, before I read Powell, and before I realized that I was expected to defend my interest—to myself and to my colleagues—in figuring out pedagogical strategies to help Native-American students whose drop-out rate is approximately 60%. I made sure to attend workshops and colloquia, and I participated in a cultural immersion program offered by the university. I worked closely with the Native-American Academic Retention Program and the Multicultural Student Center at my institution to ensure that the university's writing program would not be a stumbling block for the academic careers of Native-American students. Many of the workshops pointed out the conflicts inherent in applying academic language and literacy standards to Native-American students who try to maintain a level of autonomy and traditional values while at the same time moving within a university environment that emphasizes values mostly based on European ideologies of education. The questions that many of us asked evolved around how to provide an instructional setting in which Native-American students can acquire academic language and literacy standards while at the same time keeping traditional approaches to learning and teaching intact. In other words, we wanted to know about the social contexts in which students exhibit literacy competence, the kinds of challenges that this diverse student body faces when adjusting to academic literacy practices, and the changes and developments in literate behavior that we could expect or wanted to promote.

We experimented with high-context approaches to literacy acquisition, collaborative activities, noncompetitive learning strategies, and CMC tools to integrate student-centered learning environments into the writing program. When two of my colleagues and I presented our findings at The Minority Student Today conference in San Antonio, and at the RETAIN Conference in Flagstaff in the late 1990s, we were excited that discussions about Native-American students' academic success were taken seriously. One of the main concerns during these discussions was students' access—and often lack of familiarity—with new information technologies. How, in other words, could colleges incorporate technological literacy more successfully into the curriculum, knowing full well that technology access could be very limited, depending on where students lived, what their economic status was, and what their future career goals were.

When we discussed the possibilities for technology integration, I was reminded of my own experiences with technology. In my small farming community, computer access was not available when I grew up, and computers are still a rarity in most households. Internet access is available, but high costs discourage many from being "plugged into" the 21st century information superhighway. Staying in touch is not done through e-mail, but mostly through phone calls or visits. And even though the Internet could be used to check on livestock prices, crops, tractors, or other farm equipment, many of the people from my hometown go to the farmer's bureau, a livestock fair, or the dealer in town who will work with them on an individual basis.

The need for Internet access in such a community is limited: However, could people in my hometown use computer technologies to engage in literate activities that are currently unattainable? Could they gain knowledge that would increase crop production? How could teachers in my hometown teach technological literacy in ways that would help students achieve their career goals? And, is the infrastructure in place to support context-specific goals for technology implementation? These questions are very similar to those that our group at NAU asked about the implementation of technology to increase Native-American students' success in school and in their careers.

Because of my institution's commitment to Native-American education and to technological preparedness to meet the needs of the 21st century workforce, NAU administration and faculty were excited when, on April 18, 2000, President Bill Clinton visited the Navajo Nation. He wanted to discuss, and hopefully find ways to bridge, what he called "the digital divide"—the technology gap between rich and poor. This historic visit—the Navajo Nation had never had an official visit from a U.S. president—was seen as another promising step to expand access to new technologies, increase student access on reservation schools, and improve a currently stagnant economy. The president was hopeful that an infusion of technology and a more equitable distribution of technological wealth would address the economic difficulties that the Navajo Nation was experiencing. According to Clinton, new technologies—namely computers—would be necessary to "bridge the digital divide."

However, promising the miracles of the digital age is difficult when the mechanical age has not already arrived. I had read the 1995 landmark study by the Office of Technology Assessment, prepared at the request of the Senate Committee on Indian Affairs, where committee members had pointed out the positive developments in terms of increased connectivity which had started to take root in Native-American communities. However, the consortium also pointed out that "despite these positive signs, Native-Americans face significant barriers and challenges in realizing the potential of telecommunications. At this time, it is difficult to predict whether the ultimate outcome will be more positive than negative for Native-Americans" (p. 3). The report pointed to two possibilities for future development. An optimistic scenario showed increased access to distance education, telemedicine, and economic opportunities. But, on the other hand, the "inadequacies of rural Native-American economies and telecommunications infrastructure continue to prove too great to overcome" (p. 5).

At the time this report on telecommunications in Native-American communities was published, a government census report (1995) showed that more than 80% of the homes on Navajo Nation land had no phones, and that 30% of the Navajo Nation's residents were without electricity. When I looked through the 2000 census report, 60% of homes lacked telephone service, 32% did not have complete plumbing, and 30% did not have complete kitchen facilities. I also found out from the *2000/2001 Comprehensive Economic Development Strategy* report from the Navajo Nation Division of Economic Development that 56.1% of Navajo people lived below the poverty level, the per capita income was $6,217, and the unemployment rate was at 43.65% (http://www.nnwo.org/nnprofile.htm).

My initial research showed that there is much interest from corporate donors to alleviate the problems of the digital divide on reservation land: a $2.7 million infusion of software and technical assistance for eight Native-American colleges from Microsoft, $500,000 for online mentoring from Compaq computers, and a $30,000 satellite system that would allow some schools to connect to the Internet. Furthermore, the Bill and Melinda Gates Foundation sponsored a Native-American Access to Technology Program (NAATP) between 1999 and 2003 that was intended to provide computer and internet access to "fit tribal interests, circumstances and political arrangements" (Gordon, Dorr, & Gordon, 2003, p. 428). The foundation provided 805 computers for 161 sites and invested $9.6 million for 43 tribes in Arizona, Colorado, New Mexico, and Utah. As the report pointed out, the collaboration among several tribes in the four-corners region was a valuable experience; however, they also indicated the difficulties encountered based on "deeply embedded economic and political realities and their legacies" (p. 428). Monetary donations and technological equipment, in other words, cannot bridge the digital divide. I thought of my family in their small little rural town, and their reaction to an "infusion of technology." If the technology was imposed on them, or if it didn't help them with the immediate concerns they faced as small-time farmers, they wouldn't be interested in learning how to use it. It would be a tool that would put on dust in a corner of the house, pointed to from time to time. My family would not feel connected, and they wouldn't think that they should be connected in any more ways than they already are.

What remains a concern, then, is whether the efforts of the corporate donors indeed alleviate the gap between what Thomas Davis and Mark Trebian (2001) called the haves and the have-nots:

> First, Indian country is on one side of the digital divide that is threatening to separate the haves and the have-nots of American society in even more fundamental ways than in the past. Second, substantial parts of Indian country are aware of the importance of information

> technology to the future of Native-Americans and have made sporadic, though sometimes unsuccessful efforts to join the digital revolution. Third, the rates of success realized by tribes and Indian organizations in efforts to end the digital divide differ substantially. Some tribes have all of their schools networked and have an impressive list of Web-based accomplishments. Others do not even have basic telephone service to reservation homes. (p. 40)

I had read countless explorations about the inequities in access—which has become synonymous with "digital divide"—to new technologies in newspapers, magazines, journals, and popular or scholarly books, using various ideological, theoretical, and political frameworks. However, I knew that access was not the only problem, nor would better access alone change existing power structures that favor established economic and political systems. Barbara Monroe (2004), for example, complicated access issues in her recent work on *Crossing the Digital Divide: Race, Writing, and Technology in the Classroom*. As she pointed out, "the divide is not just racial and economic in character, but also social and discursive" (p. 29).

Monroe's comment resonated with my own ambivalence about technology's implicit and explicit value system. My early educational experiences with computers—when I was 22—were based on second-language "drill-and-kill" programs that did not encourage me to think critically about my language skills or my literate activities. Instead, these programs reinforced specific values so chillingly explained by Fred Kemp in a 1998 Computers and Writing position statement. As he pointed out, most teachers learn from those around them, following a teaching "lore" that guides them in their own practices. This lore, he argued, draws "heavily upon presumed common sense and intuition, continues to emphasize formalism, drill, lecture, and strict management of in-class behavior, the remnants of the Prussian model that had so much to do with encouraging disciplinary specialization and the incrementalization of learning in the nineteenth century, eventually to succumb to a full scale 'scientific management' of classroom instruction . . ." (Kemp, 1998). And importantly, I did not learn how to improve my writing skills by doing decontextualized grammar drills. What I did learn, however, was that my grammar was poor, and my English was not acceptable to my professors. In other words, the social function of computers from this experience was to make me aware of and reinforce my deficiencies as well as my outsider status at the university. I became dependent on the computer's discursive function of letting me know that I did not fit into a system that expected students to be proficient English speakers and writers.

Cynthia Selfe and Gail Hawisher (2000) argued a similar point in *Global Literacies and the World-Wide Web*. According to their findings, the promotion of new technologies is not always geared toward increasing a group's political, cultural, or economic independence. Instead, it can be interpreted and understood as "the devaluation or erasure of culturally specific linguistic, social, political, and religious practices" (p. 9). Discussing the "global-village myth," Hawisher and Selfe pointed out that "the Web may seem less a neutral and welcome medium for global communication than a disturbing and unwelcome system for broadcasting western colonial culture and values" (p. 9). In other words, participants in a dominant social structure's business ventures, political interests, religious and moral values, as well as educational principles are not interested in creating and promoting a plurality of perspectives, but are often participating in continuing conditions of political, economic, social, and cultural inequality. In a later work, Selfe and Hawisher (2004) used 20 case studies to reaffirm the need to learn more "about how various social, cultural, political, ideological, and economic factors have operated dynamically, in relation to each other, at various levels of influence, and over time, to shape the acquisition and development of digital literacies within people's lives" (p. 3). Stuart Selber (2004), similarly, quoted Saul Rockman to address the need for a more critical approach to implementing technological literacy in curricula and to consider the multiple factors that influence how technology is used within particular communities. As Rockman (1995, cited in Selber, 2004) pointed out:

> Ensuring that schools have the same amount of equipment will not do. Providing schools with teachers who care and know enough about how to use computers effectively will help. Installing a technology infrastructure without reason for using it does not help. Refurbishing a building and making it beautiful and safe, does. Making certain that children have enough to eat and warm clothes to wear in the winter, is also a good starting point. (p. 28).

The Navajo Education Technology Consortium (NETC), and as part of it the Education Technology Improvement Plan (ETIP), practice many of the principles addressed by Monroe (2004), Selfe and Hawisher (2004), and Rockman (1995). The consortium took the contextual and situational needs of their communities into consideration when encouraging teachers of Navajo students to "craft a unique combination of traditional Indian culture with technology" (*The Education Innovator*, 2004). The mission of NETC, according to Cedric Wyaco, technical coordinator at Pine Hill

Schools in New Mexico, is to "provide educational services on or near the Navajo Nation related to the improvement of education of children and adults through the delivery of instructional technology; to create strategic advantages by incorporating district standards and culture and to increase student achievement by identifying and promoting learning styles appropriate to the population being served" (p. 29). This consortium, with the help of the Navajo Nation, has worked toward technological connectivity for their communities while also taking into consideration the political, social, economic and cultural backgrounds of these communities. Stuart Selber (2004), in *Multiliteracies for a Digital Age*, called for a similar commitment when he argued for a rhetorically literate student who understand and practices persuasion, deliberation, reflection, and social action (pp. 146-166).

## APPROACHES TO LITERACY

It is certainly not easy to explore the various processes connected with acquiring technological literacy, specifically rhetorical technological literacy advocated by Stuart Selber (2004), especially if these processes are impacted by unfamiliar cultural and educational frameworks. I had read much about the contextual and political nature of literacy when I started to look into the Navajo philosophy of learning as part of my ongoing educational endeavor to find ways for helping students achieve their academic literacy goals. I was initially drawn to *Literacy: Reading the Word and the World*, where Paulo Freire and Donaldo Macedo (1987) emphasized that any literate activity "always involves critical perception, interpretation, and *rewriting* of what is read" (p. 36). Accordingly, they argued that "reading the world always precedes reading the word, and reading the word implies continually reading the world" (p. 35). David Barton (1994), in his call for an ecological approach to literacy, made a similar argument when he pointed out the interconnections of human activity and its environment. Literacy, in his words, "is tied up with particular details of the situation, and . . . literacy events are particular to a specific community at a specific point in history" (p. 3).

Many others in composition and rhetoric have made related arguments about the contextual, situated, and historical nature of literacy (Heath, Brandt, Lu, Fox, Street). When I researched Native-American approaches to literacy acquisition, I soon realized that discussions about the interrelated nature of literacy and life had long been integral to the Navajo philosophy of learning. According to Navajo teacher and scholar Herbert Benally (1994), for Navajos "knowledge, learning, and life itself are sacred and interwoven parts of a whole. They are holistic principles that determine the quality of each other" (p. 23). To achieve balance in life—peace of mind, physical health, emotional health, and ecological awareness—Benally argued that individuals need to follow the four principles of life that were pronounced by Mother Earth at the beginning of creation. These principles encompass

- "That which guides and directs life," or an understanding of spiritual and moral obligations.
- "Sustenance," or achieving self-reliance and an understanding of the place of work in the universe.
- "The gathering of family," or the understanding and appreciation of people.
- "Rest and reverence for all creation," or an understanding of ecology as living life and appropriate interactions with it. (p. 29)

These principles lead to a true internalization of knowledge and describe "how knowledge becomes one's life" (p. 29). Accordingly, Navajo knowledge "guides and directs life toward a state of *hozho*, more good, and *siihasin*, actualization," leading to greater spirituality and happiness (p. 31).

Benally's explorations of the Navajo philosophy of education, Freire and Macedo's comments on the connectedness of world and word, and Barton's and other scholars' emphasis on the contextualized nature of literacy emphasized for me the importance of making connections among what we learn, how we learn, why we learn, when we learn, and where we learn. Specifically, these scholars seem to tell us that knowledge about the word and the world cannot easily be compartmentalized. Instead, we learn at every moment of our lives. Accordingly, we encounter learning and literacy practices as dynamic activities that are part of a larger framework influenced by the values and perspectives of individuals and of the members of specific groups.

My experiences with school literacy were very different from Benally's description of interwoven experiences. What I learned in school was never part of what I needed to know at home. School learning was a separate entity, I did 8 years of school because it was a requirement. I continued for another 5 years because my teacher told me I should and because my parents respected the teacher. I studied for the test, and I did well on those tests because I was good at memorizing information. I knew the important dates in Austria's history, but I didn't know how to think about history in terms of current political or social events. In college, I became even better at memorizing facts and figures, but nobody encouraged me to make connections and to interweave my knowledge with the knowledge I had gained from other aspects of my life. When I finally realized that I did not have to lead multiple lives and that my fragmented selves could communicate with each other, I felt ill equipped to take on the challenge of teaching the implicit and explicit connections between the word and the world. I had not had this experience myself, and it was a long process to accept the notion of interwoven and interconnected experiences. My reluctance in my earlier research to incorporate the personal in the academic can be seen as my attempt to keep my home literacies and my school literacies as separate entities.

When I read that one of the schools chartered by the Navajo Nation, Diné College, underscores the importance of looking at the whole person and the person's position in the world, it underscored for me the importance of allowing the personal into the academic, and of making connections between school, home, work, and community. Based on Diné College's mission statement, the college applies "the Sa'ah Naagháí Bik'eh Hózhóón principles, more fully explained in Tanya Gorman Keith's (2004) dissertation, to advance quality student learning:

- through Nitsáhákees (Thinking), Nahatá (Planning), Iiná (Living) and Sihasin (Assurance)
- in study of the Diné language, history and culture
- in preparation for further studies and employment in a multicultural and technological world
- in fostering social responsibility, community service and scholarly research that contribute to the social, economic and cultural well being of the Navajo Nation. (2004, http://www.dinecollege.edu/aboutdc/mission.php)

Similarly, the Ganado Unified School District in northeastern Arizona uses as its foundations of learning a traditional Navajo Learning–Teaching model that posits thinking in the east (problem solving, deductive and inductive reasoning, and critical thinking skills), planning in the south (careers, goal setting, awareness strategies, technology, reading, writing, and math competencies), life and social awareness in the west (sensitivity to ideas, cultures and social systems, leadership skills, family and parenting skills. History, social issues, urban living, fine arts), and respect and reverence to the north (responsibility, awareness of substance abuse prevention, respect for the environment, healthful living strategies, self-respect, sense of spirituality) (see http://www.ganado.k12.az.us/offices/supt-fol-update.htm).

Unfortunately, many public educational institutions, which Deborah Brandt in (1990) called "middle-class, majority-run institution[s]" (p. 107), do not adhere to or value a context-based approach to literacy but instead often present what I experienced as a student—an abstract and largely decontextualized literacy. Despite the findings about the connections between home and school literacies (Brandt, 1990; Freire, 1968, 1973; Gee, 2004; Heath, 1983), educational institutions seem to struggle with federally and state-instituted requirements that often result in teaching to the test. For Arizona K–12 schools, Arizona's Instrument to Measure Standards (AIMS) requires school districts to complete a Declaration of Curricular and Instructional Alignment to the Arizona Academic standards annually, and it requires teachers to follow performance standards in reading, writing, and mathematics that students have to fulfill in order to graduate from high school. The "ultimate purpose of testing," the Arizona Department of Education argues, "is the improvement of student learning" (2005, http://www.ade.state.az.us/standards/aims/).

However, the Navajo Nation does not concur with the Arizona Department of Education's assessment on testing. Leland Leonard, director of the Navajo Nation Division of Diné Education, questioned the current education system that shows more than one third of schools on Navajo Nation land to fall below state or federal expectations (Peter, 2004). Not only does Leonard question state standards but he also criticizes George W. Bush's No Child Left Behind efforts. To provide better education and to alleviate federal and state-imposed standards, tribal officials in 2004 proposed to develop their own education department that would then be able to develop their own educational principles and expectations (Peter, 2004).

The restraints put on K-12 education by standardized testing, and the concerns expressed by Navajo Nation officials should encourage teachers at all levels to rethink current approaches to teaching and to testing knowledge acquisition. But, although I want to provide high-context approaches to academic literacy acquisition, I know very well that most students have been trained to study for the test. However, I still believe, strengthened by the high drop-out rates of involuntary minority students, that teaching to the test does not help students to succeed in school or to acquire critical thinking skills. I was especially concerned that old-fashioned and mostly discredited drill approaches would lead to a deterministic approach to technology. This, according to Barbara Monroe (2004), would mean "that technology is not so much revolutionary as it is evolutionary, and that evolution is inevitable, inevitably progressive, and progressively desirable" (p. 7).

Such an uncritical approach to technology, from my perspective, would only encourage students to accept current constructions of reality—including my own reality as a student that I did not fit into a system that required drill exercises for improving my language skills—without questioning the political and social forces that allow those constructions to exist. If, however, we are interested in incorporating critical technological literacy into the discussion, my argument would be, then, a high-context approach would remove the focus from the information provided by technology—the text—to how such information influences and transforms our reading of the world—the context. Similarly, I want to believe that if we look at technological literacy practices as "situated in broader social relations" (Barton, 1994, p. 41), then we can look at how social or political institutions support or discredit a particular kind of involvement with technologies. A technological consumer literacy, for example, might be supported by online business ventures; a critical technological literacy that calls for a closer examination of the rhetoric used by these businesses might be strongly discouraged by those interested in seeing these businesses succeed.

I was hoping that a focus on *critical* technological literacy would allow us to read the world from the perspective of those who are closely connected to the communities in which technological literacy practices are carried out. Without an understanding of the historical background and the social relations in which technological literacy is practiced, we might devalue the experiences of technology users and instead see them merely as information seekers who participate unscathed in the creation and proliferation of economic exploitation and political suppression. What I show next, then, is that we need to look at how the situation in which we practice technological literacy—or how thinking, planning, awareness, and respect—influences and changes us as scholars, researchers, and teachers, and also influences and changes students' perceptions on the uses and usefulness of technology.

I no longer consider technology as the all-powerful tool that will teach me how to say a grammatically correct sentence. I could move away from this perception because I worked with people who taught me differently. I started using computers in my own classrooms to implement my overall objectives of raising critical awareness about how we participate in an educational, social, political, and economic system. The tool, the computer, was only supplementary in my attempts to integrate different aspects of students' lives into their educational experiences. I used my own experiences to avoid teaching methods that did not help me understand my own positionalities, my responsibilities, and my practices as a student and as a teacher.

## HISTORIES, CULTURES, AND LITERACIES

The literacy experiences of Jolita and Mani, similar to those of others and my own experiences, are part of the histories they have been told, the histories they lived through, and the histories that are being told about them. As members of the Navajo Nation, their lives are connected to events that displaced their ancestors, disrupted social and cultural systems, and often led to forced education. They are also connected to the histories of their own families, the value that was put on traditional and school education, and the experiences their parents and grandparents tell about. Although both Jolita and Mani grew up on Navajo Nation land, their experiences and stories don't fit "neatly within simplistic notions of race, sex, class, and gender" (Lu, 1999, p. 3). Instead, their experiences, despite common histories, are complex, diverse, and multifaceted.

Mani and Jolita learned their histories from their families and their teachers. Sometimes they were told the same history; sometimes they were told a sanitized and revised version by their teachers, and an unedited and specific history by members of their families. I knew I would never know the histories that Mani and Jolita knew, but I also knew that I needed to acquire contextual information so that I could at least partially understand the stories that Mani and Jolita were telling me. I found the detailed chronology printed in the *Close Up Program* (1997) published by the Navajo Nation, Division of Education, a useful albeit general introduction to some of the past events in Navajo history and education that Mani and Jolita referenced. Both Mani's and Jolita's families lived on the Navajo Nation which spans 25,400 square miles and three states: Arizona, New Mexico, and Utah. With an estimated Navajo population of 300,000—170,000 living on the reservation—the tribe is currently the largest one in the United States The location of the reservation was decided—without input from those who were forced to live there—in 1868, when the final treaty between the Navajo and the United States was signed at Fort Sumner, New Mexico. It forced Navajos to live on a permanent reservation, and it also forced a provision on them that calls for the education—and assimilation—of Navajo children. Article VI of the Navajo Treaty of 1868 reads as follows:

> In order to insure the civilization of the Navajos, the necessity of education is admitted. Navajos pledge themselves to compel their children, male and female, between the ages of six and sixteen years to attend school. It is the duty of the agent to see that this stipulation is

> strictly complied with and the U.S. agrees that, for every 30 children between said ages who can be induced or compelled to attend school, a house shall be provided, and a teacher competent to teach the elementary branches of an English education shall be furnished, who will reside among the Indians. (*Close Up Program*, 1997, p. 55)

I had read about the U.S. government's interference in the 19th century and about the numerous broken peace treaties, but I had not known that Navajos experienced the first slave raids undertaken by the Spaniards in the 1630s. In the 1700s, they were forced to Christianize by Spanish Catholic missionaries and later on by missionaries from other faiths. I also did not know, and never thought to ask, that it took until 1924, 60 years after the "long walk" to Fort Sumner in 1864, for Navajos and other tribes to receive citizenship by the U.S. Congress. I did know that during World War II, Navajos played an important role as Code Talkers, defeating the efforts of the enemy forces to figure out what code—or language—was used to transmit messages to the allied forces. But I did not know that despite the participation in the war efforts, and despite the claim that the United States was built on democratic principles, Navajos and other Arizona tribes did not have the right to vote until 1948. As an international who had grown up with the idea that America was the home of the free and the land of the brave, I made assumptions about the democratic principles in effect in the United States. I did not stop to wonder, as Iris Marion Young would call it, whether these democratic principles encompassed all peoples of the land of the free. I was happy to learn that in the 1950s, a time that Native-American scholars have often called the "termination era," the Arizona Commission of Indian Affairs (ACIA) was charged to "study and consider the conditions among the Indians residing within the state" (http://www.indianaffairs.state.az.us/aboutus/aciahistory.html), but I was also amazed and shocked that it took until 1975, when the Self-Determination and Education Assistance Act was passed.

I chose to include these historical landmarks because they are part of the macro-structures that influence how Mani and Jolita see themselves and are seen by others. When I came to the United States, I saw myself as an Austrian who wanted to learn more about U.S. history, educational systems, politics, and literature. From conversations with U.S. nationals, I realized that they saw me as somebody from a country in Europe that only a few could locate on a map. I was the disappointing real-life specimen of characters from *The Sound of Music*. Some thought that Austria was part of the East-block communist regime. Most did not know that Austria was a powerful monarchy before World War I. And nobody knew that Austria was occupied by the British, French, Russians, and Americans for 10 years after the end of World War II. Austria's location on the border of East and West, its history as an empire, its participation in two world wars, and its depiction outside of Austria have influenced how I understand myself and how I understand the histories and cultures of others. I realized that I needed to learn more about my own histories in order to understand how Mani and Jolita are situated within specific historical, cultural, and political contexts. It underscored for me that I—similar to Mani and Jolita—am not only influenced by my histories and cultures but also by how these histories and cultures are interpreted by others.

## JOLITA: CHANGING CULTURES OF LITERACY

I met Jolita when she took one of the introductory writing courses at my current institution. We e-mailed and had face-to-face conversations, and we met in a small town on the Navajo reservation, about 90 minutes from NAU. Jolita was born in 1954—6 years after the Arizona Supreme Court conceded that Arizona Native-Americans have the right to vote, and during the "termination era" referred to by the ACIA. It was long before words such as computers, digital divide, technology revolution, or Internet access were part of anybody's vocabulary. She grew up with four sisters and four brothers, helping her parents and grandmother with the farm.

My grandfather bought the house with the small piece of land that my father inherited. Before I went to school, I helped my mom and my grandfather with the chores, planting corn and potatoes, harvesting wheat and cutting grass. I didn't know that the dialect I spoke at home wasn't acceptable for school until my sister decided to teach me how to write the German used in the classroom. Once I was old enough to go to school, I learned to speak the German of the books. But when I was at home, I went back to speaking dialect with my family and friends, and I continued to help my family with planting, harvesting, and feeding the farm animals. Knowledge I acquired in school did not become knowledge I could use in my life.

I didn't experience the conflicts that were part of Jolita's growing up. I used my dialect with my whole family. Jolita, on the other hand, spoke Navajo with her mother who only knew a few words in English. Her father, however, insisted that Jolita and her siblings were brought up the "Christian way" instead of following traditional Navajo beliefs, and that they would be educated away from home, to make sure that they had a chance to succeed in an Anglo world. Jolita wasn't sure whether her father was a visionary who knew that his children needed to be prepared differently than he was to meet the demands of a changing society—Navajo as well as Anglo, or whether he was denying his own culture and buying into the dominant Anglo society's scheme of assimilation without acknowledging the values of knowing the history and traditions of Navajo culture and life. Or, Jolita thought that he might just have wanted to preserve the health and happiness of his family.

Jolita's father grew up during a time when the voting rights of Arizona Native-Americans were ratified and when, in 1947, the Tribal Council declared compulsory education for Navajo children, ages 6 through 16. Although schooling had not been mandatory until then, many children had been forced to participate in the Anglo educational process, encouraging and forcing them to conform by speaking only English, cutting their hair, wearing Western clothes, and participating in Western religious practices. The idea behind these enforced school experiences was, according to Donna Deyhle (1991), that "the best way for Indians to become Americans was to remove their children as far as possible from the influences of their homes, families, and culture" (p. 282). However, many of the displaced Native-American peoples realized that becoming "American" did not include becoming accepted members of the largely Anglo political, social, and economic system.

I was reminded of David Barton (1994), who pointed out that access to specific literacies is restricted in all societies because "literacy involves information and idea transmission and is practiced in a context where its uses may both maintain and challenge existing social institutions" (p. 75). In other words, if the goal is to continue current power structures, only specific and limited literacy practices are sanctioned by a dominant group. Although indoctrination into Anglo educational practices was touted as a necessary step to assimilation and participation in Anglo society, it instead seemed to achieve quite a different goal, with second-class citizenship prevailing in most cases. Barton would see this as another manifestation of his belief that the "control and manipulation of literacy is pervasive and depressing in terms of what it means for people's rights and development, and their sense of personal power" (p. 78).

My understanding of how limited and prescribed literacy practices can reinforce established social, economic, political, or cultural practices, or can lead to indoctrination, is partly based on my parents' understanding of their experiences during Austria's participation in World War II in the 1930s and 1940s. The doctrines taught in school were a clear manifestation of Nazi ideology. Teachers resisting this ideology disappeared from the schools. Students who didn't start the day by raising their hands in the well-known "Heil Hitler" pose could expect a visit from supporters of the current regime in their parents' house. My parents could not claim to be Austrian; they were told that they were now part of the German Reich. History, literature, and language were taught to reinforce that the Aryan race was superior to any other race in the world. My parents will talk about these experiences when they hear about current genocides, declarations of war, or governments that deny equal rights to all their citizens. They do not use words such as restricted literacy, indoctrination, or systemic oppression; instead, they talk about how we don't learn from history, and how history is apt to repeat itself.

When I did my research on the historical and social context surrounding Jolita's and Mani's experiences, I was reminded of my parents' experiences and my parents' comments on current events. I realized that Jolita's experiences attending a Bureau of Indian Affairs (BIA) boarding school in northeastern Arizona where she was told to speak English, and to read and write in English, were part of a larger effort to provide only specific kinds of literacy to specific kinds of students. Jolita pointed out that she spent every school year in a boarding school, which meant that her parents were only peripherally involved in her educational progress. She sees her education as mostly a school education, an education that seemed to have as its requirement to become "white" (see Deyhle, 1991). As a consequence of her boarding school experience, and as a consequence of her father's insistence to practice Christianity, Jolita learned to pray to one God, speak English only, and be generally assimilated into Anglo society without being fully accepted in their world. In many ways, the school literacy she was exposed to debilitated her participation in her home community.

Jolita's boarding school experience has a long history. The first school built on the Navajo reservation was Fort Defiance Boarding school to which 12 Navajo students were "recruited" by the BIA Navajo Police Force in 1883. Between 1900 and 1910, five more boarding schools were opened on the Navajo Reservation in Tuba City, Leupp, Tohatchi, Shiprock (where former President Clinton visited), and Chinle. It was eye-opening to read Deirdre Almeida (1997), who pointed out that the values taught in boarding schools in the early 20th century were especially detrimental to Native-American women. As she pointed out, "girls were expected to learn European American techniques of childrearing, household maintenance, and food preparation" (p. 765). Thus, "schooling" destroyed the traditional roles of Native-American women and often excluded them from being full participants in Native-American communities after their return home. And although the Meriam Report of 1928 condemned the poor quality of education in boarding schools, and although the Johnson–O'Malley Act of 1934 "reaffirmed the continuing legal responsibility of both the federal government and the states to provide education for Native-Americans" (Almeida, 1997, p. 766), many boarding schools up to 1980 "were completely dilapidated and functioned more as holding pens than as schools" (p. 767).

What Jolita learned during her boarding school days, she said, was how to conform to Anglo standards. She let me know that she hated every day of her school experience but hung in there and graduated in 1972. She was convinced that she didn't learn anything at all although she has a high-school diploma. What was hardest for her during these years was her separation from her grandmother who she considered the major influence in her preschool years. When she tried out college for a semester, she realized that being away from home once again was more difficult than she first thought. She knew that she had a lot to learn again when she came back home. She started being interested in Navajo culture, participated in traditional ceremonies, and brushed up on her Navajo.

Jolita's school years overlapped with a resurgence of cultural awareness and national pride in the 1960s that, in 1968, resulted in the Indian Civil Rights Act, conferring all of the fundamental rights in the U.S. Constitution to Native-American groups. Native-Americans finally had fundamental rights such as freedom of speech, free exercise of religion, trial by jury, equal protection under a jurisdiction and its laws, and the right against unreasonable search and seizures. Furthermore, the commitment to traditional values called for major changes in Native-American educational philosophy. Navajo Nation educators tried to undo the many years of forced assimilation by emphasizing the need to teach history and cultural values to students. The first Navajo Community College, now called Diné College with various branch campuses across the Navajo Nation, was established in 1968, and classes began in 1969. The college presents itself to its students as a unique educational institution which adheres to "the Sa'ah Naagháí Bik'eh Hózhóón principles" mentioned earlier:

> As the first tribal college in the nation, Diné College is a unique institution of higher learning because it has a bicultural education mission. We combine Navajo language, history, culture and philosophy with traditional Western disciplines. The education you receive at Diné College will allow you to become successful on both the Navajo Nation and in communities beyond our four sacred mountains. (2004, http://crystal.ncc.cc.nm.us/welcome.html)

Article VI of the Navajo Treaty was signed in 1868. It took 100 years before the Navajo Nation could finally emphasize the connections between education, history, and culture, and could provide an education for its students that would allow them to make their own choices about their future careers. Jolita, however, did not experience the new push for incorporating language and culture into the teaching curriculum while she was a high school student. It was only years later, when she decided to study to become a teacher, that she became aware of some of the new approaches to education for Native-American students. Jolita's excitement about the new opportunities for Native-American students reminded me of how excited I was when I first read James Berlin's (1982) *College English* essay on the major pedagogical theories in composition studies. Berlin's straightforward explanations on how diverse approaches to the composing process and on how we define the "writer, reality, audience, and language" were instrumental in my rethinking of pedagogical and methodological approaches to teaching. My excitement about Berlin is less pronounced nowadays, but my exploration of postmodern theories, critical pedagogy, technological literacy practices, and feminist pedagogy, and my own experiences as a student have become essential in how I understand and work with students. Jolita's experiences, her realization that students would not have to go through the same educational experiences any longer, and her awareness of new educational methodologies seem to influence how Jolita defined her choice to become a teacher.

Jolita's jobs contributed to her understanding of how school literacy can be connected to home literacy, and how she can contribute to this effort. Her experiences in a Headstart office on the reservation gave her the confidence that she could attempt college again despite her long time off from school. When she went back to college 30 years after graduating from high school, she didn't have any experiences with computers because, as she pointed out, "I never thought I'd need to know how to use them." She took a computer section of the introductory composition course at the university she attended. She hoped that she would learn something that finally might help her in her efforts to help others. She did not want the kids that she would be teaching to be taught the same way she was. She knew that she was smart, and that she could do it, and she knew that the kids that she would teach needed a strong role model to see the need for school literacy in connection with home literacy. She saw her growing awareness of her own cultural background as a first step in teaching kids how to be proud of who they are.

Jolita's aims as a teacher—to make students proud of who they are and to avoid her own experiences as a student—follows the efforts of many educators who want to change the currently unsuccessful educational system. Sandra Stokes (1997), for example, viewed "the lack of culturally appropriate teaching methods and materials" as a major reason for Native-American students' high drop-out rate and negative attitudes toward school (p. 577). According to Deirdre Almeida (1997), it is women such as Jolita who will become "the keepers of their culture" because "as long as Native-American women assert their traditional rights and assume their traditional responsibility of being the central voices of their communities, Native-American nations will survive and their women's voices will remain loud and strong" (p. 769).

Tanya Gorman Keith's (2004) case study on Navajo student success and graduation rates at NAU, reminded me of my conversations with Jolita. Similar to Jolita's wish to integrate her students' experiences into school literacy, Keith showed that understanding and appreciating students' cultural backgrounds is an important aspect of success in school. She proposed a reflexive model that incorporates Navajo educational philosophy with academic educational philosophies, emphasizing "not only intellectual development, but also social, physical, and emotional development" (p. 152). Jolita seems ready to use the approach explained by Keith, an approach that takes seriously the importance of paying attention to the histories, cultures, and traditions of the diverse students in the educational system. I know that I would have benefited from such a holistic approach to education during my own school days, and my parents might have understood that a school education doesn't mean that their daughter will no longer be interested in the day-to-day activities important to them and to their friends.

## MANI: INTEGRATING CULTURES OF LITERACY

Mani and I were introduced to each other during a search committee meeting, and we started to discuss how technology could be used successfully for Navajo students. We exchanged ideas online and face-to-face, and we met at Mani's school on Navajo Nation land to talk more about her experiences with technology, her background, and her career goals. I was first introduced to the geographical area during a vacation trip out west with my brother who had never been to the United States and who enjoyed every minute of our adventure. Monument Valley Navajo Tribal Park with its 17-mile Valley Drive, many buttes and mesas, and jewelry stands, was different from anything either one of us had ever seen. We knew little about the history and current traditions, but we appreciated the land, the people, the drive, and the blue sky. When I started to work at NAU, I supplemented my tourist impressions with the impressions I received from students, colleagues, workshops, research, and multiple trips to elementary, middle, and high schools on Navajo Nation and Hopi land. When I talked with Mani and Jolita, I had moved from romanticizing the land to seeing it as beautiful but also harsh and often inhospitable and without renewable water sources. Every time I learned something new, I realized that I needed to learn more. I had learned about and been invited to traditional dances, school events, and meetings with principals. I had seen teachers work closely with their students, using Navajo and English and culturally appropriate topics to teach a subject. I had also learned about the Navajo–Hopi land dispute, an unemployment rate of close to 50%, and a poverty level exceeding 50%.

Mani lived on the Navajo Reservation all her life except for postsecondary schooling. Her mother was brought up by her paternal grandparents, spoke Navajo, and was taught "traditional values" by her grandfather who was a medicine man. Similarly, Mani's father was raised by his grandparents and learned traditional medicine from his grandfather. He owned a contracting business and is also—with four of her brothers—doing the rodeo circuit. Mani was born in 1967, the second of 11 children, 1 year before Congress enacted the Indian Civil Rights Act, and 1 year before the first Navajo Community College was established.

Mani points out that it wasn't easy growing up as the second oldest child. She had to be a role model for her younger siblings, a responsibility she took very seriously. She grew up speaking Navajo and attended a bilingual and bicultural school in Rough Rock, Arizona from preschool to fifth grade. For grades 6 through 8, Mani attended boarding school in Chinle and then Chinle Public School where she was first introduced to computer technologies. She points out that both her parents encouraged her but had little education to help their children once they entered high school. My mother, too, thought that an education was a good thing, especially for a girl from a very small rural town. She wanted to become a school teacher when she was young, but neither one of her parents appreciated her ambitions or could afford to let her go. She was needed to work off her parents' debts on their land lease, and she started working when she was 12 and finished her formal schooling when she was 14. She wanted to see me succeed, but was never quite sure what that really meant.

Mani points out that her parents also wanted their children to be successful, but success encompassed many things. They were especially pleased with Rough Rock Community School, Mani's preschool to fifth-grade school. This school sees as its purpose "to educate, enlighten, motivate, challenge, and assist in the proper cultural rearing of our Navajo children so they can be self-respecting, respectful of others, speak and practice their language and culture, and be totally functional in the Anglo society." Their objective, and responsibility, is to "teach and instill our sacred Navajo Language and way of life into each of our Navajo children who attends school here" (2002, http://www.roughrock.bia.edu/). Mani's education to fifth grade incorporated more than decontextualized "school literacy" and included knowledge of Navajo language and culture in an environment where teachers and school administrators want to teach "our children harmony with Mother Earth and Father Sky through community controlled bilingual, bicultural education" (2002, http://www.roughrock.bia.edu/). The contextualized practices of literacy used by Rough Rock Community School are an example of how a Navajo philosophy of education explored by Benally can be applied successfully in an institutional setting. Mani's experiences, in other words, illustrate how literacy as a situated practice can be implemented in a specific context where learning is understood as a holistic endeavor supported by long-held cultural beliefs.

But Mani's experiences at Rough Rock Community School were an isolated occurrence. Her schooling in the Chinle school district conformed to a traditional, de-contextualized approach to education. Although the social studies department offered some courses in Navajo history and culture, the general curriculum followed a mainstreamed approach. Emphasis was put on teaching vocational skills, and little attention was paid to students' life experiences or historical and cultural knowledge. Mani pointed out that she did not know at the time that she had been lucky to be exposed to an integrated curriculum. She only knew that she didn't like her Chinle experience and was glad when she finally graduated.

Although many of the members of the Navajo Nation consider the teaching of Navajo language and cultural values important in the education of their children, and although Mani was introduced to a bilingual, bicultural education through fifth grade, the reality for many students is often less promising. Currently, students living on Navajo Nation land attend either public schools, BIA schools, Grant and Contract schools, or Mission schools. According to the 2000 Census data, 36.5% of persons 25 years of age or older have less than a ninth grade education, 41.2% have finished high school, and only 2.9% have received a bachelor's degree or higher (Census Data). Researchers have given several reasons for the low persistence rate of Native-American students. They argue that many teachers ignore different learning and interactional styles or are not trained to accommodate these differences; they also point out that teachers use methodologies and curricula that are often not culturally appropriate or relevant. And, very importantly, schools' resources are often outdated; there are not enough books for every student, and although schools might have a computer lab, it often remains unused because the school lacks support for training teachers, for keeping the lab up-to-date, and for integrating technology in a culturally sensitive way.

After Mani's experiences at Rough Rock and Chinle schools, one of her goals as an educator was to integrate technology, culture, and the standard curriculum to ensure that education becomes relevant to students. When I met with her, she showed me some of the online teaching modules that she helped create through a technology challenge grant. The modules incorporate traditional beliefs and also satisfy the Arizona and Diné educational Standards. Lessons include Navajo Children's literature to promote listening, reading, and writing skills, beadwork to learn geometry, a family heritage lesson that employs writing, listening, presentation and general communication skills to teach children how to introduce themselves in the Diné Way, and a lesson on how to make a Navajo rug from shearing the sheep to weaving the rug introduces students to listen to a story, read with the storyteller, and read on their own. I was wondering whether Jolita would have found these lessons more interesting than the Dick and Jane stories her teachers used when she went to school.

Mani insists that technology, in addition to being integrated into a standard curriculum, needs to be used in conjunction with a student population's cultural values, reinforcing a contextualized approach to learning and literacy. Her approach is supported by researchers in computers and composition who point out the need to look closely at the macro- and micro-structures influential in students' literacy experiences (see, e.g., Blair & Monske, 2003; Monroe, 2004; Selfe & Hawisher, 2000, 2004). I also noted that it closely follows the efforts by the Navajo Nation Division of Education, the Diné Colleges, and the Navajo Nation Tribal Council which in 1984 passed a set of comprehensive education policies. As the Navajo Nation Tribal chairman pointed out, these policies

> dictate to the local schools that Navajo language is important, that Navajo culture is important, that Navajo lifestyle is important, that the preservation of our lifestyle is important. (Navajo Nation Tribal Chairman, 1985, cited in McLaughlin, 1992, p. 5)

When I started working as the Writing Program Administrator, I worked closely with Native-American Retention Programs to make sure that I considered the needs of our Native populations on campus. I wanted to make sure that the curriculum for the introductory course would incorporate materials that would provide a variety of perspectives on Native-American lifestyles and cultures. Currently, the program incorporates various readings and also includes a documentary put together by a local Native resident on the effects of snowmaking on one of the four sacred peaks a few miles south of town (K. Benally, 2005). Students watch the documentary, read about the controversy and the current court case in local papers, access and analyze a Web site connected to the debate, and talk with family, friends, and towns- and reservation people about the cultural and historical impact, the consequences for recreation in the area, and the environmental concerns about artificial snow making. It is a small effort in participating in an integrated learning experience that takes into consideration students' contextual experiences while preparing them for academic success. This small effort, however, has given voice to an issue considered important by Native-American populations across the state. Student participation has increased, and discussions have been heated. The topic has also clarified for many students the need for practicing the principles of successful argumentation we teach in the introductory composition course. They have realized that seemingly black-and-white issues have to be seen in the larger context of traditional beliefs, cultural practices, and historical and political experiences.

When Mani discusses her ideas about education, she also mentions her grandfather who was a medicine man, and who insisted that life had to be lived in balance. Similarly, Mani addresses her interest in the traditional aspects of her life and her hope that she will be able to learn more about the stories that are part of her history and her story. As David Barton (1994) put it, "current practices are based on the past. . . . They are not inevitable and unchangeable, but have developed out of past practices" (pp. 51-52).

## CURRENT TECHNOLOGY INFLUENCES

Jolita's and Mani's experiences, as well as my early experiences and my experiences as the director of a university writing program reminded me that current literacy practices, as Barton (1994) pointed out, are strongly influenced by the new technologies, radically changing the ways in which people communicate (p. 52). Both Mani and Jolita are doubtful—as doubtful as Rockman (1995, cited in Selber, 2004)—about the effects of the push for more digital technology when their families are without access to modern amenities such as running water or electricity. They are not certain what to think about President Clinton's and the corporate world's interest in the Navajo Nation's future. Actually, Jolita could not quite remember why the president visited Shiprock. She knows about the digital divide, but she also knows that her parents—similar to my parents—are quite happy without a computer in their home. She, too, would like to live her life without having to touch a mouse or a keyboard, but she knows that with her chosen career path as a teacher she needs to have some basic computer skills.

Jolita says, "I don't like them. I don't know how to use them. My teacher said to save my work on a disk, and I said 'what's a disk'? But my daughter says I have to do it. She tells me not to give up. So I keep trying. I am working on it to learn more. But I don't like them." Jolita apparently could do without being technologically literate. But she also knows that being able to use a computer is very important nowadays. Several times she points out how important her daughter's support is to her. Her daughter, she says, knows everything about computers. She helped her father set up the computer at home, a computer that Jolita never touched until this year when she needed to type her papers and send e-mail to her instructor. She also found out that she could get to the library web page and do research from home. She is determined to learn more about using computers, and although she still doesn't like them, she sees them as a necessary evil that she can no longer avoid and therefore needs to meet head-on.

Jolita's approach to computers is one of functionality. It seems to follow the 1996 definition used in the federal publication *Getting America's Students Ready for the Twenty-First Century*. Accordingly, computer literacy is defined as "computer skills and the ability to use computers and other technology to improve learning, productivity, and performance" (p. 5, cited in Selfe, 1999). What is missing from this definition, Selfe pointed out, are the social and cultural values and the contexts in which computer literacy is practiced (p. 11). In other words, Jolita seems to be at the initial stages of technological identity development, or what Nancy Barron and I refer to as "Encounter and Acceptance" (2005). At this stage, students have encountered technology but are not sure how it influences their identities and lives except in terms of better job opportunities. Jolita's approach also seems to follow Borgmann's and Feenberg's descriptions of technology users as users of value-neutral tools.

Mani's interest in computers, on the other hand, seems to acknowledge the value-based nature of technological literacy and the importance of situating computer use within a historical, cultural, social, political, and economic framework. She loves working with computers. She is not convinced, however, that President Clinton's visit revolutionized and digitized the schools. According to her, this revolution will be a slow one, and it started long before the president visited the Navajo Nation and before technology companies invested in Navajo Nation telecommunications structures. She first heard about computers in junior high school and was fascinated by the possibilities they provided for escape from everyday life. She talks about her early experience with computers—and about her experience with out-of-space technology when she watched *Star Trek* every day after school. She loved all the things that the crew could do with computers. She was very excited when she got to use computers at the age of 15. The computer course she took was a new course added to the business classes in the early 1980s at Mani's high school. She remembers that there were only four students in that class and she was one of them. Mani did some BASIC programming in the classroom and other times she was assigned to help enter data at the counseling office. She always thought computers were fascinating and fun to work with. She thought about how computer people were brilliant to come up with these machines and she dreamed of working with them someday. She was curious how a piece of machine was able to do wonders.

I was only introduced to computer technology when I left Austria and moved to the United States in the late 1980s. I had not heard of the Internet in Vienna, and I did not know what e-mail was and how it could be used until I took a class in my master's program where the instructor required e-mail of her students. I remember sitting in front of the computer, waiting for a response to a question that I had sent off 30 seconds earlier. I remember the disappointment when it took 5 minutes to get a response. And I remember slowly liberating myself from staring at the screen, commanding the computer to tell me that I have new mail.

Mani was more sophisticated about computer technology than I was. She decided to find out about the machine that could do wonders. After her high school graduation she enrolled at Diné College (Navajo Community College at the time) and received her associates degree in computer science. And in 1996, she completed a BS in computer Information systems. She learned BASIC, PASCAL, COBAL, and FORTRAN, and has been using computers for work ever since. She does not have a computer at home, but does not see this as a big problem. She can do all she wants to do on computers in her office. In 1999, Mani took a job working with the Education

Technology Improvement Project grant that trains teachers to use technology in 22 schools across the Navajo Nation. This project was initiated by the Navajo Nation school superintendents who formed the Navajo Nation Education Technology Consortium. The consortium was awarded a technology challenge grant that is intended to train teachers from 22 schools on Navajo Nation land to integrate technology successfully in the classroom.

Mani knows that her enthusiasm for computers is not shared by everybody. She knows that change is always slow. She found that out through her experience working with the grant that is designed to educate teachers to use computers so they can effectively integrate technology into their classroom instruction. This is a challenging task, she says, because there are still too many teachers out there who are still resistant to change, and change is hard. She does training every summer and introduces different types of applications, but most do not get back to the children in classrooms. Sometimes it is not the teacher's fault when the resources are limited in the school. What training she provides to the teachers is lost when they do not have access to the application they used during summer training. Other times she sends them home with copies of free applications and it doesn't get used simply because teachers do not have time to play with the programs, learn them, and use them in their classrooms.

The computer modules created through the Technology Challenge Grant (see http://www.nau.edu/%7Eifwfd/ETIP.htm and http://www.niti.org/html/models.html for more information on the grant), and the training sessions that include teachers, principals, and parents, are part of an educational philosophy that supports current explorations into literacy acquisition and current explorations into the situatedness of technological literacy. As Hawisher and Selfe (2000) pointed out in their introduction to *Global Literacies and the World-Wide Web*, we need to study "specific culturally-based literacy practices—which vary widely in their values, purposes, role, and history" (p. 15) and recognize that the web does not provide "a culturally neutral or innocent communication landscape open to the literacy practices and values of all global citizens" (p. 15). The consortium's cultural curriculum models address the need to learn about history, family, and culture while also addressing state standards. For example, one of the modules that Mani uses in her training session illustrates geometry by looking closely at the geometrical shapes used in Navajo rug weaving. She also uses interactive lessons on Native-American mathematics and culture where students learn about the Mayan calendar and the Mayan number chart. With these modules, teachers are encouraged to integrate historical and cultural knowledge into classroom practices and to emphasize the situatedness of literacy acquisition. These teachers put into practice what scholars such as Dehyle (1991), Swisher and Dehyle (1992), Lyons (2000), Berlin (1982), Street (1995), Freire (1968, 1973), hooks (1994), Keith (2004), and many others emphasized in their work, and that I was rarely exposed to in my own schooling: Productive critical learning takes place in an environment that encourages students to see themselves as part of a contextualized world.

## CONTINUING LITERACIES

I was intrigued when I found out that translated from Navajo, computers are called "metals that think." It reminded me of the different approaches towards technology that I have been exposed to in popular culture as well as academic literature. Cyberfiction strives on exploring the emotional and intellectual connections between humans and machines; HAL was certainly a thinking machine whose feelings got hurt, and there is no doubt that the Terminator's computer-operated body and mind could think beyond its circuitry. Of course it is easy to remember that we do not live in a world of fiction, and that computers most likely do not think on their own but instead are programmed to think like their programmers. Mani would agree with this sentiment. She does not believe that computers can think or do wonders. Instead, she does encourage teachers and students to use them as a tool and to become computer literate. And although Jolita thinks that computers can think and have it in for her, she is willing to fight the battle and acquire technological literacy in order to prove to herself and her family that "she can do it" and to make sure that she can get a job as a special education teacher. When I started using computers, my experiences were very similar to Jolita's. I wanted to be able to type a paper and hand it in on time. When I discovered e-mail, I enthusiastically embraced it and did not think much about the implications and consequences of using online spaces. My slow awakening to critical consciousness happened later in my career—when I was a graduate student talking to my mentor and reading about computers in the classroom. My interest in the complicated nature of technological literacy acquisition has continually grown ever since. My research, as a consequence, has always shifted, incorporating new ideas, attempting new projects, and exploring new approaches to teaching and to implementing technological literacy programs at my institution. I am still learning, and I am still wondering, as Iris Marion Young would put it, about the people I interact with, hoping to increase my understanding of how literacy is learned and practiced.

A question that I have not been able to answer fully—because of the historically and culturally situated approaches to literacy acquisition—is the following: How can we work successfully with students from hugely diverse backgrounds whose experiences with mainstream America or mainstream—if any—technology might be very different from our own or those of other students? Although I do not have the ultimate answer, what I find useful in my interactions with students is to ask them specifically about their uses of technology in their school and home environments. In a sense, I can expand on Deborah Brandt's or Shirley Brice Heath's studies on the differences between literacies used at home and in educational settings. I can include students' different uses of technological literacies in different environments (entertainment, business, politics, education, etc.), their understandings of what it means to be technologically literate, and their interest in or use for participating in the technology revolution. Certainly, I cannot engage in detailed analyses of every students' historical, cultural, political, or economic experiences. However, what I can do is learn to understand that my own histories and my place in an educational system can blind me to the needs of students in my classrooms. I can learn to listen more carefully to my students' stories that often provide useful insights into their perspectives on education, their position within an academic institution, and their home background. I can learn to contextualize—teach the word and the world—approaches to technological literacy acquisition, and—depending on the various micro- and macro-level issues addressed in the analysis of Jolita's and Mani's experiences—I can learn to see the benefits and drawback of specific technological literacies without creating a normative experience for students. My explorations of these experiences have taught me to continuously emphasize, as Tanya Gorman Keith (2004) pointed out, that "I have learned so much, but I know even less" (p. 159).

I have learned too that it's not going to be a president or members of congress who will bridge the digital divide, nor is bridging the digital divide the only issue that needs to be addressed. Instead, it is up to me and other educators to figure out how to move discussions of technology to discussions of technology's function in a normative environment and the implications such functions have in a historically, culturally, politically, and socially situated environment. I need to, as the organizers of the 2001 UC-Santa Barbara and MIT conference "Race in Digital Space" point out, "celebrate the accomplishments, while situating them against the backdrop of the challenges we still must confront" (http://cms.mit.edu/race/). These challenges, I would point out, are worth pursuing since a contextualized and situated awareness of different needs and goals can bring me closer to understanding how I can successfully teach students from various backgrounds without forcing the ideologies of educational institutions, governments, or businesses on students.

# 7

# REFLECTING

## TECHNOLOGIES AND IDEOLOGIES

> The world does not speak. Only we do. The world can, once we have programmed ourselves with a language, cause us to hold beliefs. But it cannot propose a language for us to speak. Only other human beings can do that.
>
> —Rorty (1989, p. 173)

Richard Rorty (1989) made it clear that we hold beliefs based on how we interact with others and how we use language to make meaning of the world. When I started to work on this project, I came in with a specific belief system that was based on my understanding of my position in the world, my family, cultural, social, political, and educational background, and my ideological leanings toward feminism, postmodernism, and cybertheories. I still have a specific understanding of the world, and I am still influenced by history and by current trends, prompting me, as Anais Nin (1966) pointed out, to see things as I am. I have, however, learned to value self-reflexivity, to acknowledge more fully my predilections in my approach to research, and to recognize the social nature of my literacy experiences and the literacy experiences of my case study participants. I am always struck by Elspeth Stuckey's (1991) comments in *The Violence of Literacy* where she pointed out the following:

> We are not just private individuals in whose private minds the printed word works powerful deeds. We are, to be sure, natural individuals, but we are social before we are born, and the commerce we do with liter-

> acy is always, fundamentally, social. We are arranged by our relations to literacy, to how and why literacy is produced, and to the effects of what literacy is about. The extension of these relations describes how close to the edge of survival we live. (p. 95)

When I decided to focus my study largely on involuntary minority women, I knew that I needed to pay close attention to Stuckey's commentary. It is easy to argue that it is of utter importance to the field to look at involuntary minority women since they are an underrepresented group on most college campuses where their struggles have gone unacknowledged for many years. I can also say that by foregrounding how Alba and Celie interact online, and by showing how Mani and Jolita see themselves within a larger framework, I wanted to valorize their experiences and their important contributions, and I wanted to turn them into speaking subjects and visible members of the academic community.

To an extent, I can claim that I succeeded. Alba and Celie could exhibit their literacy skills during their discussions on race and gender issues; the students involved in the group discussion could establish their authority—although it wasn't my idea of dialogic authority; and Mani and Jolita could show how important a contextualized approach to technological literacy is. But as I showed in my chapters, I also need to claim my subjectivities and my partialities. As a researcher, I have attempted to give voice to my participants. I have highlighted their achievements, and I have rooted for their success. I have interpreted their comments, and I have tried to acknowledge how my own international background influenced my analysis. I also need to claim a liability—or benefit—that most researchers encounter. I am not a U.S. citizen. I am not part of my research participants' communities, and I do not have insight into their family lives or their lives outside this study. I can't claim that I have experience living as a U.S. minority, and I can't claim that I understand the many struggles that are a permanent part of U.S. minorities. My research, similar to larger ethnographic research, was intended to create "the preconditions for research and social responsibility if only by arguing that the worlds of words separating 'us' from 'them' are not natural boundaries, but social borders that we help maintain when we refuse to travel in uncharted territory" (Brodkey, 1987, p. 42). To write such accounts, Linda Brodkey said, is an attempt "to bring stories not yet heard to the attention of the academy" (p. 48). And, "because narratives do not explain themselves, . . . ethnography must be yet another retelling, another selection and reduction of reality" (p. 48).

I found Brodkey's observations useful as a starting point for trying to understand the importance of reflecting critically on the choices that I make when moving into uncharted territory and when trying to make sense of the theories I use, the spaces I occupy as researcher, the stories I hear from my participants, and the narratives, analyses, and research accounts I write about my experiences and the experiences of my participants. The participants in this study are situated within specific theoretical and practical frameworks, some of them created by me as the researcher, and some of them created by the participants based on their own interpretations of the realities surrounding them. For instance, Alba, Celie, Jolita, Mani, and the members of the group discussion seem to use frameworks based on their own experiences with racism and discrimination and based on larger cultural, social, and political theories established about the role of involuntary minorities and women in social and educational settings. Parental influences, peer pressures, educational opportunities, stereotypes, and prejudicial behavior are part of the participants' interpretation of each other's comments and their reactions to these comments. As the researcher, it is often difficult to know why participants make certain choices when we talk to them or when they respond to specific issues face-to-face or online. Furthermore, as an alien researcher I also incorporate my own framework into the study and thus create an additional layer of interpretation to the already complex world of researcher-participant-author relationship.

Because of these complexities, I realize that it is not only important to provide readers with an overview of the components of my research project but also with an honest and critical appraisal of the processes that often get discounted or are considered outside the scope of a published work. I strongly support Gesa Kirsch and Joy Ritchie's (1995) suggestion of incorporating into our research "an extra measure of responsibility and accountability on our part," and acknowledge the "political and cultural conditions that place us in unequal power relationships with the participants of our research" (p. 25). In addition, as I suggest in this project, I need to be open and reflective about the kinds of research I engage in, the reasons for choosing specific subjects to research, and the limitations of my own perspectives and ideologies.

At the same time, it is also important to know when and how to incorporate reflection into my research without falling prey, as Powell and Takayoshi (2003) warned, to self-indulgence and narcissism (p. 155). To avoid such tendencies, it is necessary to remind myself of Min-Zhan Lu's (1999) argument for critical affirmation. In the preceding chapters, I used the personal to provide insights into how I analyze the difficulties that involuntary minority students can face in academic institutions or in finding their place in a system that has practiced exclusionary tactics for many decades. I also tried to show my own shifting perspectives and the complex nature of my own histories. I tried to underscore the need to scrutinize my own assumptions as somebody who did not grow up in the United States about race relations in the United States. I also wanted to stress that although I make assumptions about myself and those I interact with, I need to make sure that I question and analyze these assumptions and that I acknowledge the lens I use to interpret my own actions and the actions of others. Furthermore, I tried to show that my participants and I do not fit into well-defined and often reductive categories of race, gender, or class. I provided glimpses into the multifaceted styles of several participants, pointing out the complexities of their cultural backgrounds, social interactions, educational training, or family interactions and obligations.

Additionally, my work in these pages acknowledges another important caveat often overlooked by researchers. I show that it is impossible as well as undesirable, taking my cue from Iris Marion Young (1997), to explicitly and implicitly know and understand research participants. Instead, I tried to point out that my understanding needs to be created through compassionate listening and reciprocal respect of each other. I only know the realities that Alba, Celie, Jolita, and Mani wanted me to know. I can only interpret the comments that the discussions elicited, but I don't know whether these discussions are the results of long-held beliefs or newly acquired ideas. I still wonder about Bailey's position on rape and date rape, and I wonder whether the discussion led to any positive outcome. I also wonder about the impact of culture and citizenship on students' and my own view on racism and sexism, and I wonder about the influence of history on Mani's and Jolita's attitude toward technological literacy. It is this sense of wonder that encourages me to continue with my research and to ask questions that hopefully challenge assumptions about how to engage in research and how to discuss research with colleagues and students. In my earlier work, I had to establish my authority by "using disciplinary conventions in [my] writing, receiving appropriate academic credentials, participating in national disciplinary forums, and publishing in established journals" (Kirsch, 1993, p. 50). Here, although I am still confined by my authority and the authority of others, I incorporated my perspective as an alien and an academic in the United States, I reflected on my approaches to research, and I still wonder what else I could contribute in these pages that would reaffirm Min-Zhan Lu's (1999) call for "critical affirmation." But instead of considering this sense of wonder and the resulting inconclusiveness of any research as an unwillingness on the part of the researcher to commit to a traditional and well-accepted academic approach to scholarship, I hope that such work can help us move in new directions in our conception of what is valuable and acceptable research. I hope that it can move us beyond established patterns, giving credence to the work of scholars who embrace alternative scholarship such as auto-ethnography and personal narrative. Hopefully such work can prompt us to move beyond the confines of currently supported research, helping us to consider the complexities and instabilities of participant and researcher identities more fully and more openly. This approach to research, I hope, will provide a better understanding of who we are as researchers, and who the participants are in our studies. It will also allow us to admit, as Anais Nin has so succinctly expressed it,

> *There is not one big cosmic meaning for all, there is only the meaning we each give to our life, an individual meaning, an individual plot, like an individual novel, a book for each person.*

# REFERENCES


Almeida, Deirdre A. (1997). The hidden half: A history of Native American women's education. *Harvard Educational Review, 67*(4), 757-771.

Anzaldúa, Gloria. (1987). *Borderlands/La Frontera: The new Mestiza*. San Francisco, CA: Aunt Lute Books.

Barron, Nancy G. (2003). Dear saints, dear Stella: Letters examining the messy lines of expectations, stereotypes, and identity in higher education. *CCC, 55*(1), 11-37.

Barron, Nancy G., and Sibylle Gruber. (2005). *Digital media: Challenging hegemonic practices*. Computers and Writing Conference, Palo Alto, CA.

Bartholomae, David. (1987). Writing on the margins: The concept of literacy in higher education. In Teresa Enos (Ed.), *A sourcebook for basic writing teachers* (pp. 66-83). New York: Random House.

Bartholomae, David. (1988). Inventing the university. In Eugene R. Kintgen, Barry M. Kroll, and Mike Rose (Eds.), *Perspectives on literacy* (pp. 273-285). Carbondale: Southern Illinois University Press. (Original work published 1985)

Barton, David. (1994). *Literacy: An introduction to the ecology of written language*. Oxford: Blackwell.

Beale, Frances. (1970). Double jeopardy: To be Black and female. In Toni Cade (Ed.), *The Black woman* (pp. 90-100). New York: New American Library.

Benally, Herbert John. (1994). Navajo philosophy of learning and pedagogy. *Journal of Navajo Education, 12*(1), 23-31.

Benally, Klee, (2005). *The snowbowl effect*. Flagstaff, AZ: Indigenous Action Media.

Berlin, James A. (1982). Contemporary composition: The major pedagogical theories. *College English, 44*, 765-777.

Berlin, James A. (1988). Rhetoric and ideology in the writing class. *College English, 50*, 477-494.

Bishop, Wendy. (1992). I-witnessing in composition: Turning ethnographic data into narratives. *Rhetoric Review, 11*(1), 147-157.

Bishop, Wendy. (1999). *Ethnographic writing research: Writing it down, writing it up, and reading it.* Portsmouth, NH: Boynton/Cook Heinemann.

Bizzell, Patricia. (1986). What happens when basic writers come to college? *College Composition and Communication, 37*, 294-301.

Blair, Kristine L., & Elizabeth A. Monske. (2003). *Cui bono*?: Revisiting the promises and perils of online learning. *Computers and Composition, 20*(4), 441-453.

Bleich, David. (1988). *The double perspective: Language, literacy, and social relations.* New York: Oxford University Press.

Bomberger, Ann M. (2004). Ranting about race: Crushed eggshells in computer-mediated communication. *Computers and Composition, 21*(2), 197-216.

Bourdieu, Pierre. (1984). *Distinction: A social critique of the judgment of taste* (R. Nice, Trans.). London: Routledge.

Brandt, Deborah. (1990). *Literacy as involvement: The acts of writers, readers, and texts.* Carbondale: Southern Illinois University Press.

Bridwell-Bowles, Lilian. (1995). Freedom, form, function: Varieties of academic discourse. *College Composition and Communication, 46*(1), 46-61.

Brodkey, Linda. (1987). Writing ethnographic narratives. *Written Communication, 4*(1), 25-50.

Canagarajah, A. Suresh. (1997). Coping strategies of African-American students. *College Composition and Communication, 48*(2), 173-196.

Carroll, Constance M. (1982). Three's a crowd: The dilemma of the Black woman in higher education. In Gloria T. Hull, Patricia Bell Scott, and Barbara Smith (Eds.), *All the women are White, all the Blacks are men, but some of us are brave* (pp. 115-128). New York: Feminist Press.

Combahee River Collective. (1982). A Black feminist statement. In Gloria T. Hull, Patricia Bell Scott, and Barbara Smith (Eds.), *All the women are White, all the Blacks are men, but some of us are brave* (pp. 13-22). New York: Feminist Press.

Cooper, Anna Julia. (1892). *A voice from the south.* New York: Oxford University Press.

Davis, Thomas, and Mark Trebian. (2001). Shaping the destiny of Native American people by ending the digital divide. *Educause Review* (January/February), pp. 38-46.

Delpit, Lisa. (1988). The silenced dialogue: Power and pedagogy in educating other people's children. *Harvard Educational Review, 58*(3), 280-298.

de Montes, L. E. Sujo, Sally M. Oran, & Elizabeth M. Willis. Power, language, and identity: Voices from an online course. *Computers and Composition, 19*(3), 251-271.

Deyhle, Donna. (1991). Empowerment and cultural conflict: Navajo parents and the schooling of their children. *Qualitative Studies in Education, 4*(4), 227-297.

DiPardo, Anne. (1993). *A kind of passport: A basic writing adjunct program and the challenge of student diversity.* Urbana, IL: NCTE.

DuBois, W.E.B. (1982). *The souls of Black folk*. New York: New American Library. (Original work published 1903)

Eldred, Janet Carey. (2005). *Sentimental attachments: Essays, creative nonfiction, and other experiments in composition*. Portsmouth, NH: Heinemann.

Faigley, Lester. (1992). *Fragments of rationality: Postmodernity and the subject of composition*. Pittsburgh: University of Pittsburgh Press.

Flax, Jane. (1990). Postmodernism and gender relations in feminist theory. In Linda J. Nicholson (Ed.), *Feminism/postmodernism* (pp. 39-62). New York: Routledge.

Foucault, Michel. (1979). What is an author. In J.V. Harari (Ed.), *Textual strategies: Perspectives in poststructuralist criticism* (pp. 141-160). Ithaca, NY: Cornell University Press.

Foucault, Michel. (1995). *Discipline & punish: The birth of the prison*. New York: Vintage Books.

Fox, Helen. (2001). *"When race breaks out": Conversations about race and racism in college classrooms*. New York: Peter Lang.

Fox, Helen. (2004). Being an Aly. In Christopher Schroeder, Helen Fox, and Patricia Bizzell (Eds.), *AltDis: Alternative discourses in the academy*. Portsmouth, NH: Heinemann.

Freire, Paulo. (1968). *Pedagogy of the oppressed*. New York: The Seabury Press.

Freire, Paulo. (1973). *Education for critical consciousness*. New York: The Seabury Press.

Freire, Paulo, and Donaldo Macedo. (1987). *Literacy: Reading the word and the world*. South Hadley, MA: Bergin & Garvey.

Garcia, Eugene E. (1999). Chicanos/as in the United States: Language, bilingual education, and achievement. In Jose F. Moreno (Ed.), *The elusive quest for equality: 150 years of Chicono/Chicana education*. Cambridge, MA: Harvard Educational Review.

Gates, Henry Louis, Jr. (1990). The transforming of the American mind. *New Directions for Teaching and Learning, 44*, 33-44.

Gee, James P. (2004). *Situated language and learning: A critique of traditional schooling*. New York: Routledge.

Geertz, Clifford. (1973). *The interpretation of cultures: Selected essays*. New York: Basic Books.

Geertz, Clifford. (1988). *Works and lives: The anthropologist as author*. Stanford, CA: Stanford University Press.

Giroux, Henry A. (1992). *Border crossings: Cultural workers and the politics of education*. New York: Routledge.

Gordon, Andrew C., Jessica Dorr, and Margaret Gordon. (2003). Native American technology access. The Gates Foundation in Four Corners. *The Electronic Library, 21*(5), 428-434.

Graff, Gerald. (1994). A pedagogy of counterauthority, or the bully/wimp syndrome. In David B. Downing (Ed.), *Changing classroom practices: Resources for literary and cultural studies* (pp. 179-193). Urbana, IL: NCTE.

Gray, John. (1992). *Men are from mars, women are from Venus: A practical guide for improving communication and getting what you want in your relationship*. New York: Harper Collins.

Gruber, Sibylle. (1995). Re: Ways we contribute: Students, instructors, and pedagogies in the computer-mediated writing classroom. *Computers & Composition: An International Journal for Teachers of Writing, 12*(1), 61-78.

Gruber, Sibylle. (1999). Communication gone wired: Working toward a "practiced" cyberfeminism. *The Information Society: An International Journal, 15*(3), 199-208.

Guerra, Juan C. (1998). *Close to home: Oral and literate practices in a transnational Mexicano community*. New York: Teachers College Press.

Guinier, Lani, and Gerald Torres. (2003). *The miner's canary: Enlisting race, resisting power, transforming democracy*. Cambridge, MA: Harvard University Press.

Gurak, Laura J. (2004). The impact of the internet and digital technologies on teaching and research in technical communication. *Technical Communication Quarterly, 13*(2), 187-198.

Haas, Christina, and Christine M. Neuwirth. (1994). Writing the technology that writes us: Research on literacy and the shape of technology. In Cynthia L. Selfe and Susan Hilligos (Eds.), *Literacy and computers: The complications of teaching and learning with technology* (pp. 319-335). New York: MLA.

Hawisher, Gail E., and Charles Moran. (1993). Electronic mail and the writing instructor: A place in the curriculum? *College English, 55*(6), 627-643.

Hawisher, Gail E., and Cynthia L. Selfe. (1991). The rhetoric of technology and the electronic writing class. *College Composition and Communication, 42*(1), 55-65.

Heath, Shirley Brice. (1983). *Ways with words: Language, life, and work in communities and classrooms*. New York: Cambridge University Press.

Hebdige, Dick. (1979). Subculture: The meaning of style. New York: Methuen.

Hill, Paul. (2004). Date rape is the new student fear. *Times Higher Education Supplement, 1659*, 7.

hooks, bell. (1981). *Ain't I a woman: Black women and feminism*. Boston, MA: Southend Press.

hooks, bell. (1984). *Feminist theory: From margin to center*. Boston, MA: Southend Press.

hooks, bell. (1989). *Talking back: Thinking feminist, thinking Black*. Boston, MA: Southend Press.

hooks, bell. (1992). *Black looks: Race and representation*. Boston, MA: Southend Press.

hooks, bell. (1994). *Teaching to transgress: Education as the practice of freedom*. New York: Routledge.

Hourigan, Maureen M. (1994). *Literacy as social exchange: Intersections of class, gender, and culture*. Albany: State University of New York Press.

Houston, Marsha. (1992). The politics of difference: Race, class, and women's communication. In Lana F. Rakow (Ed.), *Women making meaning: New feminist directions in communication* (pp. 45-59). New York: Routledge.

Jessup, Emily. (1991). Feminism and computers in composition instruction. In Gail E. Hawisher and Cynthia L. Selfe (Eds.), *Evolving perspectives on computers and composition studies: Questions for the 1990s* (pp. 336-355). Urbana, IL: NCTE.

Jordan, June. (1985). *On call: Political essays*. Boston, MA: Southend Press.

Keith, Tanya Gordon. (2004). *Sihasin, meaning of graduation to Navajo college students at Northern Arizona University: An interpretive case study*. Unpublished doctoral dissertation, Northern Arizona University, Flagstaff.

Kemp, Fred. (1998). The way we will have become the future (histories) of computers and writing. A position statement. *Kairos, 3*(2), http://english.ttu.edu/kairos/3.2/coverweb/statements/kemp.html

Kirsch, Gesa E. (1993). *Women writing the academy: Audience, authority, and transformation*. Urbana, IL: NCTE.

Kirsch, Gesa E., and Joy S. Ritchie. (1995). Beyond the personal: Theorizing a politics of location in composition research. *College Composition and Communication, 46*(1), 7-29.

Kramarae, Cheris, and Paula Treichler. (1990). Power relations in the classroom. In Susan L. Gabriel and Isaiah Smithson (Eds.), *Gender in the classroom: Power and pedagogy* (pp. 41-59). Urbana: University of Illinois Press.

Lee, Spike. (1989). *Do the right thing*. Forty Acres and a Mule Filmworks, Brooklyn, NY.

Lightfoot, Sara Lawrence. (1980). Socialization and education of young Black girls in school. In Sari Knopp Biklen and Marilyn B. Branniga (Eds.), *Women and educational leadership* (pp. 139-163). Lexington, MA: Lexington Books.

Lorde, Audre. (1978). Litany for survival. *The Black Unicorn: Poems*. New York: W.W. Norton.

Lorde, Audre. (1990). Age, race, class, and sex: Women redefining difference. In Russell Ferguson, Martha Gever, Trinh T. Minh-ha, and Cornel West (Eds.), *Out there: Marginalization and contemporary cultures* (pp. 281-287). Cambridge, MA: MIT Press.

Lu, Min-Zhan. (1992). Conflict and struggle: The enemies or preconditions of basic writing. *College English, 54*(8), 887-913.

Lu, Min-Zhan. (1994). Professing multiculturalism: The politics of style in the contact zone. *College Composition and Communication, 45*(4), 442-458.

Lu, Min-Zhan. (1999). Redefining the literate self: The politics of critical affirmation. *College Composition and Communication, 51*, 172-194.

Lunsford, Andrea. (2000). Refiguring classroom authority. In Michael A. Pemberton (Ed.), *The ethics of writing instruction: Issues in theory and practice* (pp. 65-78). Stamford, CT: Ablex.

Lyons, Scott. (2000). Rhetorical sovereignty: What do American Indians want from writing? *College Composition and Communication, 51*(3), 447-468.

McCracken, Nancy Mellin. (1992). Gender issues and the teaching of writing. In Nancy Mellin McCracken and Bruce C. Appleby (Eds.), *Gender issues in the teaching of English* (pp. 115-125). Portsmouth, NH: Boynton/Cook.

McLaren, Peter, and Tomaz Tadeu da Silva. (1993). Decentering pedagogy: Critical literacy, resistance and the politics of memory. In Peter McLaren and Peter Leonard (Eds.), *Paulo Freire: A critical encounter* (pp. 47-89). New York: Routledge.

McLaughlin, D. (1992). *When literacy empowers: Navajo language in print*. Albuquerque: University of Mexico Press.

McKee, Heidi. (2002). "YOUR VIEWS SHOWED TRUE IGNORANCE!!!": (Mis)Communication in an online interracial discussion forum. *Computers and Composition, 19*(4), 411-434.

Monroe, Barbara. (2004). *Crossing the digital divide: Race, writing, and technology in the classroom*. New York: Teachers College Press.

Mortensen, Peter, and Gesa E. Kirsch. (1993). On authority in the study of writing. *College Composition and Communication, 44*, 556-572.

Navajo Education Technology Consortium carries Native American culture overland via the internet. (2004). *The Education Innovator* 27.II (July 19). http://www.ed.gov/news/newsletters/innovator/2004/0719.html

Navajo Nation Division of Education. (1997). *Close Up Program*.

Navajo Nation Washington Office. (2004). *2000/2001 Comprehensive Economic Development Strategy*. http://www.nnwo.org/nnprofile.htm

Nin, Anais. (1966). *The diary of Anais Nin, 1931-1934* (Edited and introduced by Gunther Stuhlmann). New York: Harcourt, Brace, Jovanovich.

Ogbu, John U. (1988). Literacy and schooling in subordinate cultures: The case of Black Americans. In Eugene R. Kintgen, Barry M. Kroll and Mike Rose (Eds.), *Perspectives on literacy* (pp. 227-242). Carbondale: Southern Illinois University Press.

Peter, Zsombor. (2004). Navajos want say in how they educate their own students. Gallup Independent. http://www.gallupindependent.com/120704navajos.html.

Powell, Katrina M., and Pamela Takayoshi. (2003). Accepting roles created for us: The ethics of reciprocity. *College Composition and Communication, 54*(3), 394-422.

Powell, Malea. (2002). Listening to ghosts: An alternative (non)argument. In Christopher Schroeder, Helen Fox, and Patricia Bizzell (Eds.), *Alt/Dis: Alternative discourses and the academy* (pp. 11-22). Portsmouth: Boynton/Cook.

Regan, Alison. (1993). "Type normal like the rest of us": Writing, power, and homophobia in the networked composition classroom. *Computers and Composition, 10*(4), 11-23.

*Rethinking Schools*. (2002). Special Collection on Bilingual Education. http://www.rethinkingschools.org/special_reports/bilingual/resources.shtml.

Rich, Adrienne. (1977). *Claiming an education*. Speech delivered at Douglass College, Rutgers University, New Brunswick, NJ.

Rockman, Saul. (1995). In school or out: Technology, equity, and the future of our kids. *Communications of the ACM, 38*(6), 25-29.

Rodriguez, Richard. (1981). *Hunger of memory: The education of Richard Rodriguez*. Boston: David R. Godine.

Romano, Susan. (1993). The egalitarianism narrative: Whose story? Which yardstick? *Computers and Composition, 10*(3), 5-28.

Rorty, Richard. (1989). *Contingency, irony, and solidarity*. Cambridge: Cambridge University Press.

Rose, Mike. (1989). *Lives on the boundary: The struggles and achievements of America's underprepared*. New York: The Free Press.

Rough Rock Community School. (2002). Main page. http://www.roughrock.bia.edu.

Royster, Jacqueline Jones. (2000). *Traces of a stream: Literacy and social change among African American women*. Pittsburgh: University of Pittsburgh Press.

Schroeder, Christopher, Helen Fox, and Patricia Bizzell. (2002). *AltDis: Alternative discourses and the academy*. Postsmouth, NH: Boynton/Cook Heinemann.

Selber, Stuart. (2004). *Multiliteracies for a digital age*. Carbondale: Southern Illinois University Press.

Selfe, Cynthia. (1999). *Technology and literacy in the twenty-first century*. Carbondale: Southern Illinois University Press.

Selfe, Cynthia L., and Gail E. Hawisher. (2000). *Global Literacies and the world-wide web*. New York: Routledge.

Selfe, Cynthia L., and Gail E. Hawisher. (2004). *Literate lives in the information age: Narratives of literacy from the United States*. Mahwah, NJ: Erlbaum.

Selfe, Cynthia L., and Richard J. Selfe, Jr. (1994). The politics of the interface: Power and its exercise in electronic contact zones. *College Composition and Communication, 45*(4), 480-504.

Shaughnessy, Mina P. (1977). *Errors and expectations: A guide for the teacher of basic writing*. New York: Oxford University Press.

Sheridan-Rabideau, Mary, Rachel McLaughlin, and Jennifer Novak. (2002). Contested knowledge: Technological literacies and the power of unacknowledged disciplinary investments. *Computers and Composition, 19*(3), 347-359.

Siegel, Deborah L. (1992). Legal definitions of sexual harassment must be broad. In Carol Wekesser, Karin L. Swisher, and Christina Pierce (Eds.), *Sexual harassment* (pp. 143-151). San Diego, CA: Greenhaven Press.

Smith, Beatrice Quarshie. (2004). Teaching with technologies: A reflexive autoethnographic portrait. *Computers and Composition, 21*(1), 49-62.

Stabile, Carol. (1994). *Feminism and the technological fix*. New York: Manchester University Press.

Star, Susan Leigh. (1991). Invisible work and silenced dialogue in knowledge representation. In I.V. Eriksson, B.A. Kitchenham, and K.G. Tijdens (Eds.), *Women, work, and computerization* (pp. 81-92). North-Holland: Elsevier Science.

Stokes, Sandra M. (1997). Curriculum for Native American students: Using Native American values. *The Reading Teacher, 50*(7), 576-584.

Stone, Allucquère Rosanne. (1995). *The war of desire and technology at the close of the mechanical age*. Cambridge, MA: MIT Press.

Street, B. (1995). *Social literacies*. Longman. London.

Stuckey, Elspeth. (1991). *The violence of literacy*. Portsmouth, NH: Boynton/Cook.

Swail, Watson Scott, Alberto F. Cabrea, and Chul Lee. (2004). *Latino youth and the pathway to college*. American Higher Education Report Series, Educational Policy Institute.

Swisher, Karen, and Deyhle, Donna. (1992). Adapting instruction to culture. In Jon Reyhner (Ed.), *Teaching American Indian students* (pp. 81-95). Norman: University of Oklahoma Press.

Takayoshi, Pamela. (1994). Building new networks from the old: Women's experiences with electronic communication. *Computers and Composition, 11*, 21-36.

Tannen, Deborah. (1990). *You just don't understand: Women and men in conversation*. New York: William Morrow.

Taylor, Todd. (1998). The persistence of authority: Coercing the student body. In Todd Taylor and Irene Ward (Eds.), *Literacy theory in the age of the internet*. New York: Columbia University Press.

Tatum, Beverly Daniel. (1992). Talking about race, learning about racism: Application of racial identity development theory in the classroom. *Harvard Educational Review, 62*, 1-24.

Tatum, Beverly Daniel. (1997). *Why are all the Black kids sitting together in the cafeteria?: And other conversations about race*. New York: Basic Books.

Turkle, Sherry. (1984). *The second self: Computers and the human spirit*. New York: Simon & Schuster.

Turkle, Sherry. (1996). We are moving from modernist calculation toward postmodernist simulation, where the self is a multiple, distributed system. *Wired*, 149+.

U.S. Census Bureau. (1995). Government census report. http://www.census.gov.

Wallace, Michele. (1993). Negative images: Towards a Black feminist cultural criticism. In Simon During (Ed.), *The cultural studies reader* (pp. 118-131). New York: Routledge.

West, Cornel. (1993). *Race matters*. Boston: Beacon Press.

Wilson II, Clint, and Félix Gutiérrez. (1994). Advertising: The media's not-so-silent partner. In Irene L. Clark (Ed.), *Writing about diversity: An argument reader and guide* (pp. 792-803). New York: Harcourt Brace. (Original work published 1985)

Young, Iris Marion. (1997). Asymmetrical reciprocity: On moral respect, wonder, and enlarged thought. In *Intersecting voices: Dilemmas of gender, political philosophy, and policy*. Princeton, NJ: Princeton University Press.

# AUTHOR INDEX

# SUBJECT INDEX

Printed in the United States
76162LV00005B/88-114

9 781572 737044